The Agency Secret ™
by Anthony Gindin

Copyright © 2024 Anthony Gindin. All rights reserved.

No part of this book is to be reproduced in any form without the express written permission of the author. Excerpts that are less than 200 words in length may be quoted with clear attribution to the author.

Published by Kindle Direct Publishing 2024.

THE AGENCY SECRET

TREAT YOURSELF LIKE A CLIENT

Proven Models to Transform & Scale
the World's Most Talented Agencies

ANTHONY GINDIN

TABLE OF CONTENTS

PREFACE
The Agency Secret ix
The Purpose of this Book xi

YOUR LEADERSHIP
1: The Illusive Magic Bullet 3
2: A Look in the Mirror..5
3: Putting Yourself First..9
4: Becoming Intentional 13

THE 4 LEVERS OF AGENCY™
5: Focus (Generalist vs Specialist)............................. 23
6: Retention (Long-Term vs Short-Term)....................... 29
7: Positioning (Industry vs Persona).......................... 37
8: Offer (Strategy vs Execution)................................ 45

THE CLIENT PERSPECTIVE
9: Start with Who 55
10: Your Perceived Value.. 61
11: Process Alone is Not a Differentiator 65
12: Results & The Unique Mechanism 69
13: The Strategic Offer... 75
14: The Client Transformation Story™......................... 81

MARKET POSITIONING

15: The Layers of Market Positioning............................ 89
16: Harpoons & Helicopters..................................... 97
17: Acquiring Objectivity 103

SYSTEMIZING REPEATABLE GROWTH

18: Aspirational Positioning.................................. 109
19: Growth Modelling... 113
20: Reverse Engineered Metrics.............................. 117
21: The "In-House Client" Model............................. 123

CULTURAL SOCIALIZATION

22: Sum of the Vectors 131
23: Leaders Create Tension 135
24: The Big Announcement....................................139

COURAGE & COMMITMENT

25: Your Investment Strategy 145
26: The Emotional Cycles of Change.......................... 153

> "I'm always amazed by how stupid
> I was just two weeks ago."
>
> Alan Weiss, Consultant

PREFACE

The Agency Secret

The Purpose of This Book

THE AGENCY SECRET

I know what you're probably thinking.

The "cobbler's children have no shoes." Agencies don't take proper care of themselves. I've heard all this a million times before...

And this idea of treating yourself like a client...

This is nothing new. This is no secret.

To which I have an incredibly simple response:

Then why aren't you doing it?

Why is your agency not growing the way you'd like it to grow?

Why are you not as profitable as you'd like to be?

Why are you even reading this book?

You see, the secret is not the *idea* of treating yourself like a client. And it's certainly not telling everyone that you're going to do it either.

The secret is actually doing it.

But don't worry, this book isn't (really) about how to treat yourself like a client. In fact, that concept only accounts for about 3.7% of what you're about to read. Yet, it's a concept that underpins everything.

Because if you can't learn how to put yourself first, you'll have a hard time accomplishing any of the other strategies outlined in the coming pages.

With that in mind, welcome to *The Agency Secret.*

THE PURPOSE OF THIS BOOK

This book is for the agency principal who's looking to systemize repeatable growth. Who not only wants to grow – but wants to grow more profitably. Who's willing to change everything to get there.

It's a meditation in the strategic decisions most agencies face as they grow, providing both philosophical thought structures and practical frameworks to help you navigate those decisions.

My goal is to help you build an agency that consistently achieves 20%+ year-over-year growth, while working to achieve a 20%+ net profit margin. Or as I like to call it: 20/20 vision ;)

To do that, I've structured this book as follows:

In Part 1 – **Your Leadership** – we discuss the mindset required to lead people through a successful agency transformation.

In Part 2 – **The 4 Levers of Agency™** – I share a framework designed to help you take a step back and conduct a deep assessment of your core business model.

In Part 3 – **The Client Perspective** – we discuss your dream client, the results you can produce for that client, the unique mechanisms you'll use to do so, and how you can productize and package that to develop a more effective approach to new business.

In Part 4 – **Market Positioning** – we discuss how to create an intentional and magnetic client journey, then pull your dream clients through that journey.

In Part 5 – **Systemizing Repeatable Growth** – we look at the systems required to make all of this work. How you develop an accurate sales forecast, reverse engineer it to create an effective marketing plan, then operationalize treating yourself as an actual client.

In Part 6 – **Cultural Socialization** – we discuss the importance of leadership and culture when looking to install a new vision, implement new systems, and get everyone pulling in the same direction. Because if you can't do this properly, you may as well light this book on fire and throw it out the window ;)

In Part 7 – **Courage & Commitment** – we discuss the mental and emotional stress that comes with trying to grow an agency, considering when (and how) you should invest in your company and the importance of being emotionally aware.

To get the most out of this book, please understand upfront that we won't be walking through a single master model that every agency should follow – because every agency is unique.

Instead, we'll walk through a collection of different frameworks – jumping from one to the next – all of which are designed to help you analyze your current situation, map your ideal future, then create a plan to get there.

As you read this book, I hope an abundance of great ideas rain down upon you.

Write them down as you have them.

Don't be a silly goose.

From this moment forward, I want you to dream big.

> *"If your dreams don't scare you, they're not big enough."*
>
> Ellen Johnson Sirleaf

I'm thrilled to have you along for this journey.

I appreciate the respect you're showing me in reading this book.

And I sincerely hope you find value in the coming pages.

If after reading this book, you want help implementing any of its strategies, you can visit **AnthonyGindin.com** to get in touch and request a meeting.

> "The most successful hunters have more patience than hunger."
>
> Scott Z. Burns, Playwright

PART 1

YOUR LEADERSHIP

The Illusive Magic Bullet

A Look in the Mirror

Putting Yourself First

Becoming Intentional

CHAPTER 1
THE ILLUSIVE MAGIC BULLET

Today, we see an abundance of online marketing "gurus" who sell us a book (or online course) promising some magic system to supercharge our growth. Sellers of snake oil, who flood the market with their mysterious (and often useless) "magic."

I feel the need to point out the obvious here.

There is no magic system.

There never was. There probably never will be.

If you've been searching for a magic bullet this whole time, then I hate to be the one to break it to you... but building the right system is about putting in the work.

Something most agencies have never actually done – because they're too busy working on their clients, without taking the time to work on themselves.

The first time I was given the opportunity to completely rebuild a new business program, I was working at an agency called Think Shift. We spent an entire year designing, building, testing, and perfecting that system before it was fully operationalized.

We grew by 63% the following year. I was astonished by the results.

We put in the work – and that's when the magic happened.

Fast-forward to the present, where my most recent client just reported 117% revenue growth since completing our work together. More than **doubling their total revenue** within a single year.

In both cases, we didn't achieve those numbers by shifting around our sales and marketing tactics or plugging in some magic new lead generation system. We did it by putting in the work to transform the agency from the ground up.

By having the awareness to recognize our shortcomings - then the courage to do something about it.

A process that can only begin in one place.

By taking a hard and honest look in the mirror.

CHAPTER 2
A LOOK IN THE MIRROR

Let's start with a story about you.

About the typical agency trajectory.

Reaching that first million (in annual revenue) almost killed you, but you made it. Fighting an uphill battle with little to no credibility to stand on.

Your second million was no walk in the park either – standing on the credibility of your one big client (and a few small others).

From there, your continued growth comes in bursts. An ebb and flow that lacks consistency, while fueling your worst fear: that if one thing goes south, you'll have to let people go. The people you love and worry about every day.

But as you continue to grow, things begin to feel more stable for the first time. It's nice.

A delusion you take comfort in.

Yet, most of your large new business opportunities still come directly through the agency principal – or through the magic of a single, irreplaceable salesperson.

A system that is inherently unscalable.

Meanwhile, it takes your staff every minute of every day (and then some) to service the clients you have, leaving little room for them to assist with your new business efforts.

You've debated whether you should "niche down" and specialize further, to have a more targeted approach in your sales and marketing – but you don't want to turn away any high-paying clients. So, you leave the door open, nice and wide, for whoever wants to come in.

Due to the width of this doorway, you've likely acquired a somewhat random collection of clients over time – from different industries, with differing needs. And this makes it hard to dive deeper into any one specific industry or area of focus.

So, paralyzed by indecision, you coast along, continuing to collect whatever comes through the door. All the while aware that your lack of specialization is making it harder to attract new clients – simply because you don't have a sharp enough hook.

Your brand isn't positioned to resonate deeply enough with any one specific type of client. And you can't say, with a straight face, that you have a well-oiled sales and marketing machine.

To achieve that next level of growth, you know something needs to change – but what?

Perhaps you know what needs to change, but you're currently stuck in the (never-ending) process of attempting to make that change. Getting hung up in the details, spinning in circles, drowning in indecision.

There are too many cooks in the kitchen. And too many paths to follow. So you coast along, doing what you do, likely to achieve the same level of results over time.

CHAPTER 3
PUTTING YOURSELF FIRST

"...place the oxygen mask over your nose and mouth before assisting others..."

I remember the first time I heard this; five years old, sitting on an airplane, fascinated by the entire process. I remember thinking to myself... why would they tell a parent to put their own mask on before helping their children?

Instinctively, that didn't sound quite right.

But I quickly came to realize: the logic was undeniable.

If the parent doesn't put themselves first and ensure they have enough oxygen to operate, they won't have the ability to help anyone else, including their own children.

The same is true for agencies. If you want to grow, thrive and operate like a well-oiled machine, you need oxygen. You need to put yourself first.

Yet, agencies operate in a high-pressure environment where, traditionally, the demands of the client always take precedence – leaving little room to ever put yourself first.

Thus, you don't take proper care of yourself.

You often spend your days underwater, trying to find those moments where you can come up for air. Where you can pause, take a deep breath, and find the open space to take a deeper look at your business.

And by failing to create that space, you fail to treat yourself with anywhere near the same level of care, attention or strategic thinking that you do your clients.

So, although flight attendants have been warning you about this your entire life, you continue to put the mask on others, before adequately securing your own mask first.

And one day, you just might find, that you're running out of oxygen.

Our journey begins with a simple choice.
To put your own mask on before assisting others.
To become your own most important client.

A line of logic that is, again, undeniable.

Ask yourself this:

What would happen if you treated yourself with the same level of care, attention and strategic thinking that you do your most important client?

CHAPTER 4
BECOMING INTENTIONAL

Continuing down our path of introspection, let's consider another important question:

What kind of leader do you want to be?

Leadership is to the individual...
What culture is to the organization...
What brand is to the customer...

All of which can be designed (and aligned) as you see fit.

Through the process of becoming more intentional.

The single biggest mistake leaders make is a failure to (truly) be intentional about every aspect of the business. Most things just happen as you go. Yet, most leaders believe they're more intentional than they actually are.

In psychology, this is called "the overconfidence bias" where people believe they're better at something than they actually are. A coping mechanism that occurs naturally when facing consistent stress.

It's therefore important that we open our minds to the possibility that we're not as intentional as we probably could be (myself included).

A former colleague of mine, Dr. Balaji Krishnamurthy, once wrote:

Intentionality is the ability to step out of your body (metaphorically) and examine yourself, asking the question, "How would I like things to be?" Then returning to your body to make those things happen.

Most companies exist as what they are, not what they could be.

That gap between what you are, and what you could be, can only be closed with intentionality. Through the recurring process of stepping back to examine your business, asking yourself how you'd like things to be – then making it so.

Incremental vs Transformational Change

In a 2020 study by KPMG, research showed that 92% of CEOs believed their business model was in need of significant change within the next three years. A separate study found that 83% of business owners felt their organizations needed significant change at the present moment.

As the world races by, faster and faster each year, most organizations feel they're behind in some way; overwhelmed by the abundance of new technologies, platforms and practices in the marketplace today.

What holds most organizations back is the way they approach change: tackling problems one by one, year after year, at a pace of change that fails to mirror the world around them.

This practice is known as incrementalism.

If you're like most companies, you pick a few big things to tackle each year, such as updating your brand, creating a new website, or implementing a new accounting software. But at year's end, you've only completed two out of three things.

So you carry the unfinished one over to next year, add two new things – then repeat the same process. Perpetually working through a never-ending cycle of attempted change. One that never sees you reach any destination.

It's a hamster wheel to nowhere town.

This short-term thinking also results in an organization that never steps into full alignment. That can never fire on all cylinders, because only a portion of those cylinders are working properly at any given time.

If you have a growing list of things you want to change, incrementalism is not the answer.

> *"Incrementalism is innovation's worst enemy."*
> Nicholas Negroponte

In a world where 83% of organizations feel they're currently behind, there's only one way to ever get ahead. At some point you need to blow everything up, then put it back together again.

To take a step back, analyze every aspect of your business, map out a holistic change process (that brings everything up to date and into alignment) then execute those changes within a single fiscal year.

The first time you do this can be labeled a **"transformation year."**

The start of what I call a **Recurring Transformation Cycle™** where you repeat this process once every 3-5 years to stay ahead of the curve. Or more accurately, to keep pace with the world around you.

Your first transformation year will be the most demanding and resource-intensive, due to the backlog of things you'll need to change. But it needs to be done.

Once complete, you can then transition back to an incremental approach for 3-5 years until your next transformation year.

But the second (or third) time you work through a transformation year, the process becomes faster and lighter – due to the previous work already completed. Because you'll be working from the foundations of a fully aligned organization.

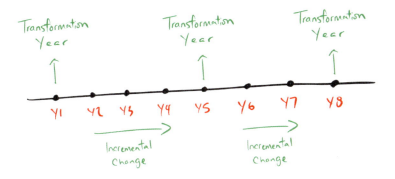

This book provides the frameworks required to work through your first transformation year. Frameworks you can return to, in subsequent transformation years, to streamline this process.

It's how the best organizations stay ahead of the curve today - by consistently futureproofing their businesses.

In the next section, we'll discuss where that transformation process begins. With a deep assessment of your core business model.

PART 2

THE 4 LEVERS OF AGENCY™

Focus

Retention

Positioning

Offer

THE 4 LEVERS OF AGENCY™

The mistake most agencies make, when looking to reach the next level of growth, is a failure to look deep enough – under the hood – at their core business model.

They look at their sales systems, their marketing tactics, and sometimes have the courage to put their brand positioning on the table for review. Never quite looking deep enough at the fundamentals of what they do, who they do it for, and whether that model is even scalable.

The 4 Levers of Agency™ is a framework I use to help agency principals assess their current business models against their future aspirations. It codifies four obvious questions that lay the foundations of your agency business model, when looked at in concert with each other.

Focus: Are you a generalist or a specialist agency?

Retention: Do you pursue long-term relationships or short-term project engagements?

Positioning: Do you target clients by industry or persona?

Offer: Do you lead with strategy or execution work?

GENERALIST ⟵ 🎯 ⟶ SPECIALIST
FOCUS

LONG-TERM (AOR) ⟵ 🔄 ⟶ SHORT-TERM (PROJECT)
RETENTION

INDUSTRY ⟵ ✛ ⟶ PERSONA
POSITIONING

STRATEGY ⟵ [S/E] ⟶ EXECUTION
OFFER

Think of each as a lever you can pull in either direction. A continuum between two options, upon which you must find the sweet spot. The point that best sets you up for profitable growth.

Over the next four chapters, we'll assess each of these in detail.

CHAPTER 5
FOCUS

Generalist vs Specialist

You've been pondering this one since the dawn of your agency (and are likely still pondering it today). How narrow should your focus be? Are you all things to all people?

Or are you just one thing, to only one specific audience.

GENERIC POSITIONING

A mentor and former colleague of mine, David Baker, once told me a powerful story. He was at a conference listening to Tim Williams speak about brand positioning and how most agencies are all things to all people, simply because they're scared to turn away new business.

So, they leave the door open, nice and wide, for whoever wants to come in.

Tim put up a slide showing examples of various agency websites, pointing out that many of them were almost identical in terms of their brand position and messaging.

As David sat there listening, he suddenly came to a disturbing realization: his agency was on that slide.

David sunk deeper into his seat, taking a moment to process what he was seeing and hearing. Yet, almost immediately, he realized Tim was right. His agency's brand position was indeed very similar to the other agencies on that slide.

Yikes.

There he sat, having a lightbulb moment as he watched his agency be (gently) criticized for being too generalist, too generic.

Following the presentation, David approached the stage, waiting at the bottom of a small metal staircase for Tim to step down. The two chatted briefly, developing a relationship that ultimately led to a paid consulting engagement.

The first time David told me this story, I thought to myself, "Now that's a brilliant sales tactic." Although I shouldn't assume Tim's intent, I suspect he had gathered a list of agencies that would be in the room that day, then put a group of them on a slide as an edgy tactic to engage them in conversations. A tactic that clearly seemed to work rather well.

But what's most important about this story is the accuracy of Tim's observation. Most agencies have not only similar, but incredibly generic positioning.

The Generalist

In one of my favorite TV series, *Mad Men*, we followed Don Draper, watching him navigate the daily challenges of a classic, old-school, generalist mega-agency.

The goal was to have one massive client in each major industry. An airline, a car brand, a beverage brand, a cigarette brand, etc. A model that made sense then, and is still used today, by the world's largest agencies.

If you can somehow achieve this model, go nuts. You'll make lots of money. But for the rest of us, we must find a realistic way to build and grow our agencies.

The problem is that many small to medium-sized agencies are working to achieve this same model, whether intentionally or not. Over time, they naturally pick up a somewhat random collection of clients (from different industries) and find themselves feeling stuck in a 'full-service' agency model with a client base that's all over the map. Making it harder and harder to specialize over time as the client base only gets more and more diverse.

So, facing what they feel are limited options, they think to themselves, "Let's just get all the biggest clients in our city," or, "Let's get one big client from each major industry."

Lines of thinking that all lead to the same result: **a random collection of clients with very few things in common.**

A lazy approach of going with the flow, taking what you can get, and failing to find the courage to specialize or differentiate.

You land a big client here, a big client there, and for some time feel as though you're riding a wave. Then one day, your luck starts to run dry. Suddenly, landing clients becomes harder than ever before. You find yourself stuck on the infamous "growth plateau."

What the hell happened?

Your generalist stance isn't resonating with any one specific type of client. It's like fishing with a wooden nub on the end of your rod, instead of a sharp metal hook. How are you supposed to catch anything?

For this reason, a generalist stance can limit your growth potential.

The Specialist

Just as the generalist stance tends to limit growth, the specialist stance tends to boost growth (when well executed). The challenge is in determining how specialized you need to be; in finding your sweet spot along that continuum. Because you can also become too specialized when focusing on too small a market to succeed.

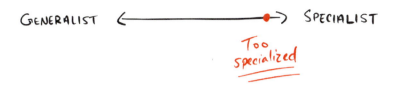

People come to agencies seeking expertise they don't already have (in-house). The deeper and more specific that expertise is, the more likely they will want to hire you. A simple and universal truth that took me decades to fully accept.

In all the years I did agency new business (which I'm technically still doing today), I often grew frustrated with clients who believed industry-specific experience was the most important component in agency selection. You and I both know that it's often not overly important. In fact, there's often great benefit in coming to the table with a fresh outside perspective.

But the truth is – when it comes to landing most clients – you'll get more meetings if you can demonstrate deep expertise that is relevant to their business. The deeper and more specific, the crazier the client would have to be to not want to meet with you.

I'll break this down into one really long sentence…

A specialist position enables you to focus on a smaller set of things, so you can develop deeper expertise in those areas, have a more focused brand position, establish greater credibility, produce highly relevant content, get more meetings with your dream clients, and (hopefully) produce better results for the clients you acquire, due to the ever-increasing specificity of your expertise.

FIELD OF EXPERTISE

A family doctor is an expert who tends to build a roster of patients organically. Their collection of patients is typically built from people who are geographically close to their physical office and have therefore selected them out of convenience.

On the other hand, a doctor who specializes in hip replacement surgeries is likely (1) quite rare compared to the generalist practitioner and (2) in higher demand. They likely have a waiting list of six months or more, just for the initial consult.

The demand outweighs the supply due to the scarcity of the expertise provided. And the scarcity of the expertise provided is due to its high degree of specialization.

Specialization is about stepping away from commoditization. When you focus on a certain type of client, or producing a certain type of result - you become a scarce resource.

Harder to replace and less interchangeable.

CHAPTER 6

RETENTION

Long-Term (AOR) vs Short-Term (Project)

The second lever is about client retention. Do you pursue long-term relationships, such as Agency of Record (AOR)? Or do you pursue short-term project-based engagements?

LONG-TERM (AOR) ⟵ RETENTION ⟶ SHORT-TERM (PROJECT)

Most agencies dance on a line between the two. You desire large AOR clients, but accept projects when you can get them. Leading to a "take whatever we can get" mindset, which breeds a lack of intentionality around what type of work you want, how you pursue it, and how you structure your business to service it.

It's important to understand that each service model puts drastically different demands on your business.

Long-Term (AOR) Relationships	Short-Term (Project) Engagements
• Slower sales cycle • More resource-intensive sales process • Bigger return over time (per account) • Less need for constant new biz wins • Breeds a generalized brand position, due to acquiring AOR clients across different industries • Requires a broader service set	• Faster sales cycle • Repeatable/efficient sales process • Smaller return (per account) • Constant need for new biz wins • Breeds a specialized brand position, because you can focus on a specific service or result • Enables a focused service set

Now, let's examine these differences in a little more detail.

Pursing AOR Clients

Typically, the fastest way to scale your agency is to consecutively acquire large AOR clients, then keep and grow those accounts over time. Easier said than done, as this approach comes with various inherent challenges.

First, pursuing AOR clients often requires your participation in an RFP process; the most resource-intensive method to land a new client. A process that is often unpredictable and unfair.

Second, is the scarcity of opportunities. For the average agency, there's no steady stream of AOR opportunities landing on your desk each month. They don't grow on trees. They don't rain down from the sky. And most agencies would be lucky to compete for a handful of AOR opportunities in any given year.

Third is having to maintain a broad internal talent pool. Large AOR clients typically want an agency that can do everything in-house, which inevitably requires you to become a 'full-service' agency.

> I once lost a massive AOR pitch to Bayer where they told us that – we were the best choice – but they chose McCann because they could negotiate better media placement rates. McCann had a large in-house media team, whereas we farmed out media to a partner agency.

Creating a chicken-and-egg scenario where you have to employ a wide enough range of skill sets to attract and secure those large AOR clients. Yet, you also need enough AOR clients to keep all those people busy every day. Creating a web of operational challenges around staff utilization, efficiency, and ultimately - your profitability.

So, while pursuing AOR clients may be the ideal for many agencies, it's important to note the significant challenges that come with this approach – including the cumbersome RFP process, the scarcity of opportunities, and having to maintain a broad internal talent pool.

THE CUMBERSOME RFP PROCESS

Having spent many years on the client side myself, I know firsthand that many RFP processes are rigged from the start, with a pre-selected winner, forcing a collection of agencies to jump through hoops when there was no chance of winning in the first place.

I want to take this moment to apologize for the role I played in doing this to several agencies (during my time on the client side). It's totally inexcusable.

As agencies, the things we do to secure AOR clients are quite staggering. Thus, I want to briefly jump down a specific rabbit hole to answer an age-old question:

Should you do spec work?

Most agencies today can be found proudly proclaiming, "We don't do spec work." Yet, when the right opportunity presents itself, you abandon that stance in a hurry – as you should. But first, let's differentiate between two different types of spec work:

1. Spec work that is **requested by the client** as part of a pitch process.

2. Spec work **you choose to do on your own** to stand out.

If spec work is a requirement, just to participate in an RFP process - you should consider that a red flag (unless of course it's Nike or some other opportunity of a lifetime).

But when the right AOR opportunity comes your way, you would be silly not to consider using spec work as a mechanism to stand out and obliterate the competition.

In my career, I've personally closed over $43 million in agency new business and financing. And I could probably cut that number in half if I'd have arrogantly stuck to a 'no spec work' policy.

For example, I once closed a $15 million contract in Switzerland, as an extreme underdog, up against much larger and more impressive international agencies. We did this by doing two things...

First, a bold approach. Our response to the RFP was telling the client that the RFP itself needed to be thrown in the trash because the goals they had set were not only unachievable, but that they were focusing on the wrong problem entirely. We then showed them the real problem and provided a thoughtful roadmap to tackle that problem over multiple years. An approach that demonstrated strong leadership, while clearly differentiating us from the other agencies and ultimately winning us the business.

Second, we did some impressive spec work. My classic go-to strategy was to produce a video that would make the client cry. I would tell our video producer that we have one simple goal: tears. If the client cries, we win. Pretty straightforward, although difficult to achieve.

In the final pitch, we dimmed the lights and played a three-minute video. After turning the lights back on, two of the seven team members on the client side were visibly wiping tears from their eyes – moved by the narrative we presented in the video. By the vision we had laid out for their future,

> and how we captured their purpose in a deeper and more meaningful way than they had seen before.

So yes, I do champion the strategic use of spec creative, when used sparingly in the right situations. But I also share this story to demonstrate how resource-intensive the pursuit of AOR clients can become. In the above example, we flew a large team of people round trip from Canada to the UK, then again to Switzerland just a few weeks later. And we had our best people working on this for weeks.

In summary, the pursuit of AOR clients is a long and involved process that requires impressive confidence and significant investment – with no guarantee of results.

Now let's consider the pros and cons of pursuing project work.

Pursuing Project Work

Typically, it's easier to sell project work, mainly because it's a smaller commitment for the client. This means you can land clients faster and more consistently. However, due to the short-term nature of this work, it also creates a revolving door of clients that come and go.

This creates two issues. First, your new business efforts must remain constant to keep new clients coming in the door. Second, every new client requires onboarding and discovery - just to get things rolling.

Yet, a project focus also enables you to be more specific with what you do. You can provide a smaller set of services or offers. You can maintain a narrower range of internal skillsets. And you can be more specialized in how you position your brand.

E.g., "We make websites for professional sports teams."

That greater degree of specialization enables you to develop deeper and deeper expertise as you go, due to the repetitive nature of the work. Which also enables your teams to become faster and more efficient over time.

You then start to produce better results for your clients, due to the learning that takes place when you try to produce the same results, over and over, with different clients. And by producing those better results, you can tell stories that are more specific, impressive and relevant to your dream clients.

But I want to be clear: my intent here isn't to make a project focus sound better than an AOR focus. In fact, over time, a project focus may be harder to maintain due to the relentless need to consistently land new clients – paired with the possible exhaustion of your client base.

At the very least, you should always look to have some form of long-term retention offer. Whether it's AOR, retainer, subscription or some other model.

> *It's important to note here that I'm using "AOR" as a blanket term to refer to any long-term retention model.*

> *Any model that enables you to retain clients over the long-term and earn consistent revenue.*

For most agencies, it's about finding a balance between the two (AOR and project).

It's the ability to have long-term partnerships that sustain the business, while using project work as a mechanism to get new clients in the door. In that scenario, project work not only fills in revenue gaps, but serves as a tool to reel new clients in before finding the opportunity to convert them into long-term AOR relationships.

A simple and obvious process I call The Magnetic Client Journey™.

An approach I'll cover extensively throughout this book.

Becoming intentional about the balance between AOR and project work serves to define a core component of your agency business model; one that impacts how you position yourself to the market, how you structure the services you offer, how you staff your agency, and ultimately – how you work to acquire new clients.

Yet, of the four levers, this is often the most overlooked.

CHAPTER 7

POSITIONING

Industry vs Persona

The third lever is about positioning; do you define your market by industry or persona?

Here we start with the most fundamental strategic question of all:

Who is your dream client?

From my experience, the agencies who can clearly answer this question without hesitation – tend to grow faster than those who cannot.

There are two general ways you can define your dream client.

The first is by industry; by a group of people or companies that have already been clearly defined. You could purchase a list of these people today.

The second is by persona; by a group of people you have defined in your own way, based on certain characteristics such as their problems, goals or behaviors.

Industry positioning enables you to build a targeted list of your dream clients, while persona positioning enables you to connect with those clients on an emotional level.

SPLIT FOCUS TARGETING

Once upon a time, I led business development at a talented, multi-national ad agency.

When I got there, the agency had just completed a merger between two companies.

- Company A was a full-service ad agency focused on AOR clients in the agricultural sector.

- Company B was a project-focused consulting firm; doing leadership and culture work with CEOs across a variety of sectors.

Following the merger, the executive leadership group mandated that we focus our efforts on two different markets. The first (defined by industry) was agricultural clients. The second (defined by persona) was CEOs who were eager to drive change.

For well over a year, I aggressively debated this strategy. What was the point of merging these two companies if we were going to maintain a split focus? This required us to essentially run two different new business programs, to two very different audiences.

It was one thing to split our focus between two audiences, but another to define each audience in such different ways. One was defined by industry alone (agriculture) while the other was defined by persona alone (CEOs eager to drive change).

Eventually, the executive leadership group came around to what was likely an inevitable decision: to drop the split focus and merge these two concepts into one (simply defined as agricultural companies looking for broader strategic change).

Yet, looking back, I wouldn't trade this experience for anything. I developed a deep understanding of the differences between marketing to an industry versus a persona.

With industry, we could build a clear list of companies and market to them directly (through email, LinkedIn, conferences and more).

Whereas with persona, it was more about understanding their pain points, developing strong messages that resonate, and positioning those messages strategically – whether through inbound or paid search.

The moral of my story is this: I came to understand that you always need both.

One layered on top of the other.

Industry positioning is a clear and practical approach to defining your target market. By defining an industry, you can quickly build a large audience for marketing activities.

Yet, most agencies struggle to define this. Initially, this is because most agencies grow up acquiring a diverse range of clients, across different industries, and lack the courage to specialize in any one industry (for fear of alienating others). Furthermore, most agencies view the concept of 'industry' incorrectly and through too narrow of a lens.

Where strategy comes into play is in defining **the scope of industry positioning;** finding the scope that is most appropriate for your specific agency. It can be as broad as B2B or B2C. As specific as agriculture (which includes several sub-industries). Or as narrow as hair salons in Dallas.

The Scope of Industry Positioning

BROAD ←——•———————•———————•—→ NARROW
          B2B   Ag   Hair Salons in Dallas

Because with any of the above-mentioned groups, you could purchase a list of them tomorrow. You could find industry associations that represent these groups, conferences that cater to them, and so on. You simply have to map out the available options, then find the courage to select one – and lean into it.

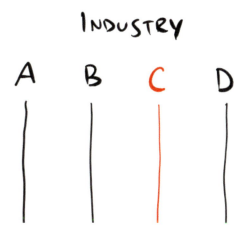

This is where most agencies fail. They worry too much about the clients they have, fail to find the courage to be more specific with their industry positioning – then coast along, business as usual, trying to cater to everyone.

Persona positioning – on the other hand – enables you to connect with your dream clients on a deeper level by speaking to their pain points.

But... without industry positioning, persona positioning is nebulous. It leaves you speaking to a person who might exist across multiple industries.

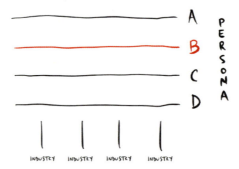

Industry positioning is weak without persona positioning. And persona positioning is too broad to be effective on its own.

Therefore, your dream client sits at the intersection between the two.

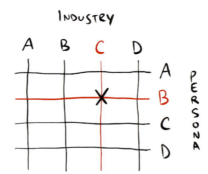

You need industry positioning to be precise and practical, building a large list of potential clients that you can market to directly. This is required to scale.

You need persona positioning so you can develop emotional connections with your audience by demonstrating a deep understanding of their unique problems. This is required to book meetings.

Most agencies are held back by a generalist position that fails to lean into either, never mind both.

Leaning into one makes a substantial difference.

Leaning into both is where the magic happens.

Finding Your Sweet Spot

In summary, effective positioning sits at the intersection between industry and persona.

Finding that sweet spot enables you to speak to a very specific type of client – while telling a very specific type of story. And within that combination, you can demonstrate such a unique and specific level of understanding, that your dream client would have to be crazy to say no to a meeting with you.

Finding that sweet spot is the foundation of great positioning.

CHAPTER 8

OFFER

Strategy vs Execution

The fourth lever is about what you offer (and what you sell). Do you lead with strategy or execution-based services?

Let's start with the fundamental premise: that strategy-first agencies can demand higher prices where execution-first agencies cannot.

It's why most agencies are always looking for ways to make their services appear more strategic. Because: not only do strategic services command higher prices – they also typically earn higher margins.

However, a profitable client-agency relationship isn't determined by the mere provision of strategic services. Rather, it's determined by how a client first engages with your agency. The initial service they seek – strategy or execution – will shape the trajectory of your partnership.

So, within the blend of strategy and execution work (that all agencies provide), what do you choose to lead with? What is your spearhead? And what do clients first come to you for?

Looking Through the Client Lens

Every client wears different lenses when looking for different things. Just as one might select reading glasses to read the newspaper, versus sunglasses to cut the glare while driving – clients too, switch lenses based on their objectives.

When hunting for strategy, they'll reach for their 'strategy glasses' - which bring into focus only those firms who highlight their strategic capabilities. Everything else will be out of focus, blurring into the background - and likely going unseen.

In contrast, when looking for execution or implementation work, clients look through a different lens. One that limits their range of focus to firms that are positioned around the specific service they're looking for.

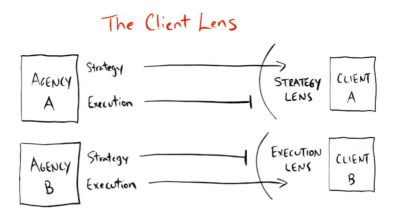

The reality is: every agency provides both strategy and execution work. The question is: what type of client relationships do you want?

Clients who hire you for strategy, will want you for implementation work. But clients who hire you for implementation, may never want you for strategy work.

What's important here is how a client first enters your domain. What was the client looking for when they first engaged you? And what was the first thing you did for them? The answer to these two questions will dictate the parameters of a client relationship.

I invite you to sit down and make a list of your two best clients and your two worst clients. Then answer the above two questions for each of them. I'd be willing to bet that your best two clients first hired you for strategic work, while your worst two clients first hired you for implementation.

When you attract clients looking for strategy, they see you as a partner and respect you as a leader. As such, they're open to paying higher prices.

When you attract clients looking for execution, they see you as a vendor and expect you to take orders. As such, they expect competitive pricing.

As a recurring theme throughout this book, we'll discuss the various ways you can position yourself more strategically to enhance your perceived value. One of the most important levers you can pull within your core business model.

ALIGNING THE 4 LEVERS

Decades ago, as a young man, I spent almost 10 years working in the music industry as an R&B music producer (while running a small agency). And I won't lie to you: I was pretty hip-hop happenin' back then.

Whereas today, I drive kids to soccer, am passionate about gardening, and enjoy a good quiche ;)

During my time as a producer, I would pull together various artists, compose and record original music, then sit in the studio, in front of one of those big mixing boards – mixing the different tracks until we achieved that magical moment where the sound came out just right.

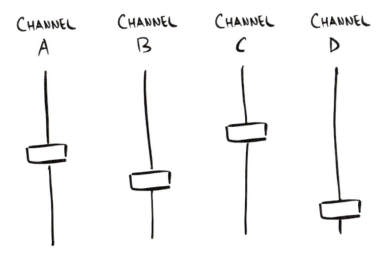

That moment where I would press play, hear it, and have to stand up and step back from the mixing board – because I could taste the perfection. Tears flowing down my face every single time.

The 4 Levers of Agency™ is like that big mixing board.

But this mixing board isn't used to adjust the volume of different tracks in a musical composition. It's a mixing board that defines the future of your agency.

If your growth (or profitability) isn't where you want it to be – your quest begins here.

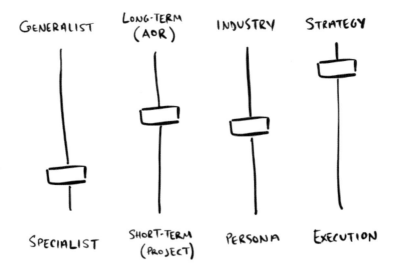

The 4 Levers of Agency™ represent the fundamental set of interdependent variables that define your agency business model. You must adjust each of them, in concert with each other, until they're fully aligned, and you've found the right mix.

And when you get that mix just right, perhaps you can have a little cry of your own.

**Listening is the most powerful practice you
can perfect – in both life and business.**

PART 3

THE CLIENT PERSPECTIVE

Start with Who

Your Perceived Value

Process Alone is Not a Differentiator

Results & The Unique Mechanism

The Strategic Offer

The Client Transformation Story™

CHAPTER 9
START WITH WHO

In one of the most influential business books of our time – *Start with Why* – bestselling author Simon Sinek argues that organizations should start with a clear sense of purpose around "why" they do what they do, rather than focusing on what they do or how they do it.

Although I fully agree that organizations should be driven by a clear purpose, I don't believe this is where one should "start." Rather, I believe the imperative is that all organizations *Start with Who*.

Everything you do, and everything you are, needs to be centered around a clear understanding of who you do it for. The audience, persona, dream client, stakeholders – or whatever you prefer to call them.

Your customer's voice is like a compass. It's what you must follow, if you want to get where you're going.

Businesses succeed by understanding and fulfilling customer needs. By creating value in the mind of the customer and establishing enduring relationships. A process that requires you to start with who; to start with the simple duty of listening to your customers.

The Great Train Robbery

In 1903, a motion picture called *The Great Train Robbery* became the first film to include credits that were shown at the beginning of the film.

From 1903 to the late 1990s this practice continued as the industry standard, where viewers were forced to spend anywhere from two to ten minutes watching a long list of names dance across the screen, slowly, one by one – often to music. The director, the producers, the actors, and a bunch of other random people that the viewers don't care about.

The only reason these credits were shown at all, never mind at the beginning of the film, was because the people making the films were trying to make a name for themselves with other filmmakers. It was never intended to serve the audience. It was intended to serve the people who made the film.

For over 90 years, the people making films were well-aware that the people watching their films didn't want to see this – but they did it anyway.

For over 90 years! It's rather insane, really.

It wasn't until the early 2000s when we saw this practice disappear from most movies.

Fast-forward to today, where many of the "blockbuster" films brought to theatres are two to three hours long, despite research showing that the average viewer prefers a film less than 90 minutes in length.

All of which demonstrates an industry that continuously fails to listen to its customers.

So, what does listening look like?
You can of course interview your dream clients to build personas, and you should. But personas are static. Once crafted, they remain unchanged for years on end, like old photographs amidst the rapidly evolving backdrop of a changing world.

I therefore want to share a practice you can layer on top of your personas; a practice I've been applying successfully for more than two decades.

Customer Inclusion

Customer inclusion *is the process of including (actual) clients in (select) strategic decisions.*

Let's say you're in the middle of redefining your business model, repositioning your brand, or working through any other big strategic decision. This is the perfect time to pull in your best client and ask for their input.

Because there's no better advisor on the planet.

> **DATING ADVICE**
>
> Terrence, 24 years old, is hoping to find his life partner. He recently went on a string of first dates with women he grew to admire. Each time, he would get home, brimming with excitement, and dance around his kitchen thinking, "This might be the one!"
>
> He'd call up one of his friends and go on and on about how amazing she was. Yet, he wasn't able to arrange a second date with any of them.
>
> Thus, he was left defeated, wondering to himself, "What am I doing wrong?"
>
> In this situation, who could give him the most useful advice?
>
> Other men, who are more successful in the dating world?
>
> Or, women in his life (who he already knows and trusts) that are similar to the types of women he is interested in dating?

If you want to understand how to serve your clients better – or build an agency that attracts more of your dream clients – why not go straight to the source?

Take your best client for lunch or hop on a quick phone call. Tell them they're one of your best clients and that you want to attract more clients like them. Explain the concept of customer inclusion as a mechanism to inform key business decisions. Then tell them what you're working on and ask for their input.

Your client will react positively to this. They'll recognize the respect you have for their opinions, appreciate your acknowledgment of their strategic acumen, and feel more connected to your agency – working to only deepen your client-agency partnership.

But most importantly, you'll obtain valuable insight that could only come from your dream client. You can understand what they value most, then work to build an agency around delivering that value. And the journey toward this understanding begins with a simple yet profound approach: learning to listen.

Listening is the most powerful practice you can perfect – in both life and business.

CHAPTER 10

YOUR PERCEIVED VALUE

Perceived value is the worth a person assigns to a product or service, based on their own (unique) perception of how valuable it is to them.

HERE'S THE LOGIC

Clients pay more for services they consider to be strategic.

This is because they perceive them as having higher value.

Therefore, by leading with strategic services, you can enhance your perceived value.

When you attract clients looking for strategy, you establish the foundation to charge higher prices from day one. You set a baseline to be respected as a strategic leader. And you avoid being seen as an order-taker, which leads to a more fruitful client relationship over time.

You therefore want to attract clients who are looking for strategy.

But what does it really mean to "lead with strategy?"

First, let's acknowledge that the most common agency services (creative, websites, content, etc.) will continue to become more and more commoditized over time. A trend of rapid devaluation that will only speed up with the adoption of new AI tools and other platforms.

This flood of new do-it-yourself tools (like Canva) will continue to get better, enabling everyday people to design great creative, build great websites, produce impressive videos, or create whatever else they need. And your clients are well aware of this.

We are therefore now drifting into what will become a highly saturated space, with increasing competition from new low-cost providers, that will force price-based competition and continue to erode agency pricing and margins over time.

Yikes.

> Three years ago, I hired a small agency to build my consulting website (for a modest fee). Yet three months ago, I replaced that website with a new one that I built (by myself) using a website-building platform called Kajabi.
>
> The new website is faster, looks better, works better, and I have total control over every item on every page. I also don't have to call an agency every time I want to make a big change, which represents a huge improvement to my workflow.
>
> In all fairness, I do have a background in graphic design and UX planning, but the point remains the same: the days of paying an agency $40,000 to build a 'beautiful website' are close to being over.

But that doesn't mean the demand for skilled website development agencies is going anywhere. It only begs the question – what value can they provide?

Clients will no longer place high strategic value on the standard, commonplace services that most agencies list on their websites – regardless of what you name those services.

We must instead find new ways to enhance our perceived value by re-engineering those services to (legitimately) deliver greater value to our clients.

Not by giving the same services a fancy new name. Please stop doing that.

You can enhance your perceived value. But only after you elevate your actual value.

For example, you can continue to "build websites." Or you can turn that same service into something of greater value. You could build e-commerce sites that are optimized for conversions. Or you could build high-performing sales funnels. Both of which are strategic services, connected to measurable business results, that demand a higher price.

> When I built my original consulting website, I paid a small local agency $3,500. And there's no reason to pay much more than that for a website today. The website they built was beautiful and served its purpose for many years.
>
> I also cofounded an ecommerce company in 2020, which we took public on the CSE (Canadian Stock Exchange). When we hired an external agency to build that ecommerce platform, we paid them $250,000. It was a Shopify site, built on an existing template, with some heavy structural modifications.

> The $250,000 price tag for the e-commerce site is over 70 times more than the $3,500 paid for the consulting website. And although it was a more complex build, it was nowhere near 70 times more complex or time-consuming.
>
> Both projects took around three months. And both agencies were around the same size, with similar teams that had comparable skill sets.

What's important about this story is that in both examples, the service being provided is website development. A service that – whether it's for a basic website, an e-commerce site, a sales funnel, or whatever – still requires most of the same people and skill sets.

Any website development agency can level up their people and skill sets to shift from website development to a more strategic, higher-value service, through a bit of intentionality, professional development and perhaps the hiring of one new expert to lead the team. Then they could start charging 70 times more for the work they do ;)

A line of thinking that can be applied to any set of services. It's about answering the question, "How do we use the same set of people and resources to deliver greater value to our clients?"

You do this by listening to your dream clients, understanding what they value most, then re-engineering what you do to deliver that value.

CHAPTER 11

PROCESS ALONE IS NOT A DIFFERENTIATOR

Too many agencies pitch their 'unique' process as a selling point, even though most agencies follow some variation of the exact same process. That process typically includes the following generic stages:

Learning is a process where the agency gathers intel from the client. Planning is a strategy phase, where the agency formulates their thinking into a plan. Development is an execution process, where the agency builds something for the client. And launch is where the client approves something, so the agency can deploy or deliver it.

And in some cases, the agency sticks around to help optimize what has been done. A process that is often shown as a circle, indicating how the agency intends to push the client back into more work ;)

There's nothing unique about this process, regardless of what you name the process itself or the components within the process. If you ever find yourself walking clients through this process in a sales meeting - please stop.

It's good to have a process. But process alone is not a differentiator.

> ### AGENCY LINGO
>
> In addition to spending over a decade agency-side, I spent over nine years client-side, working with some of the best agencies in the world. And I credit my expertise in agency new business to my time spent as a discerning client.
>
> During that time, it was a common practice, in each company I worked at, to gently make fun of the agencies

we worked with. Specifically, to make fun of their unique "shtick" as it related to the terminologies they used to describe what they do. We'd have an absolute field day.

I once remember ending a call with a UK agency who told us they needed to "take this up to the nest" to "have a think." Now, they did have an upper floor in their office, that they referred to as the nest. But we still thought it was hilarious.

To this day, when I speak with colleagues from that time period, we still end calls by stating that we're going to "head up to the nest to have a think." We then die laughing. It's an inside joke that never gets old.

I share this story to make a point: that your clients are just as smart as you are. They already know that every agency has the same basic process. And they might be having a laugh, at your expense, if you try to assign a fancy nomenclature to that process.

I remember one agency that called their process "The 360 Client Matrix." It was a circle that said, "Learn, Plan, Grow."

Riveting stuff, really.

I vividly remember them structuring the agenda for our first call around a walk-through of the steps in their process. During the call, I remember putting the phone down and running to the kitchen to grab a banana.

Upon my return, I put the phone to my ear just in time to hear them transitioning from the "Learn" phase into the "Plan" phase. I was on the edge of my seat, literally, as I considered running back to grab a second banana.

> Let's just say – in the end – we opted not to work with that agency.

My point is – don't be that agency.

You can increase your perceived value by re-engineering your services to be more strategic. But you can't increase your perceived value by trying to make the standard agency process sound more interesting than it really is.

At the end of the day, what clients really care about are **results.** And your process is only important when it shows your dream client how you can help them achieve those results.

When it shows that you have a **unique mechanism** for doing so.

CHAPTER 12
RESULTS & THE UNIQUE MECHANISM

What key results do you produce for your clients?

Sadly, most agencies lack a clear answer to this question.

From the agencies I've worked with, very few could confidently answer this question when I first met them. And for those who could, somewhat vague answers were provided, such as, "We help our clients grow." Which could basically mean any one of a hundred different things.

Clients want an agency they can believe in; an agency that can lead them up the mountain. And to engender such belief, you'll need a compelling story that includes two key components:

1. The (big) **end result** that you'll help them achieve.
2. The **unique mechanism** you'll use to do so.

The end result should tie directly into a common measure of company performance, such as revenue growth, profitability, customer satisfaction or employee engagement. Doing this will help you make a more compelling case to the "economic buyer" within the organization (i.e., the person who controls the budget).

The unique mechanism is a framework, philosophy or - yes, even a process - that shows how you'll lead them toward achieving that end result. It demonstrates how organized you are and that you have a proven system, built around achieving a specific end result.

Clarifying your results and unique mechanisms can become the basis for not only service design and productization, but also for your brand positioning.

Yet, most agencies are a far cry away from having either of these things clarified. Instead, most agencies lead with (1) a vague positioning statement; (2) a list of commonplace services; and (3) a non-differentiated process.

> ### THE AGENCY SEARCH PROCESS
>
> Julie is searching online to find and hire a new agency.
>
> Having reviewed many already, she lands on yet another agency's homepage and reads their leading message, "We Deliver Big Ideas That Matter."
>
> She has no thoughts or feelings about this.
>
> She clicks through to the services page to find a standard set of services that include Marketing Strategy, Brand Identity, Website Development, and Social Media Management. She reads on to learn about the agency's process, that includes four phases:
>
> - Discovery
> - Strategy
> - Development
> - Launch

Finally, she clicks through to view a set of case studies, finding some beautiful brands and websites. She thinks to herself: this agency must have some good designers.

This is the 27th agency website she's reviewed in the past three days. She suddenly finds herself lost, halfway through a case study, as her interest begins to wane. Her mind wanders to what she might make for dinner that night.

Without a moment's hesitation, she closes the website tab, never to return again. She leans back in her chair, settling into a deep and satisfying yawn. Her arms raise up to the sky as her big yawn shifts into a deep and even more satisfying stretch. She mutters under her breath, "Ohhhhh, that's a good stretch."

Suddenly, she perks up in her chair, thinking to herself... I could make a stir-fry tonight! It's been a while. Wait... I could even use that frozen shrimp sitting in the back of the freezer.

Yes, a shrimp stir-fry. Perfect!

The clock strikes 3 pm as she climbs out of her chair into a standing position, surprised by how dizzy she suddenly feels. Looking at all those agency websites sure made her feel sleepy.

She wanders over to the kitchen in search of more coffee. She can barely remember how many agency websites she just looked at or what any of them said. They were just all so similar, blending together into a big soup of nothingness.

Mmmm, soup.

> Her gaze turns toward the pantry as she wonders what she might snack on before returning to her desk. Could that last can of tomato soup still be in there?

I know this story because it was once me. In my 9+ years client-side, I put out countless RFPs, researched hundreds of agency websites, reviewed countless proposals, and so on. The experience described above is what I typically went through every time I looked for an agency. It was a painful, mind-numbing task. Just one after another with little to no differentiation.

THE WELL-POSITIONED OFFER

> After a satisfying bowl of tomato soup, Julie returns to her desk, hot cup of coffee in hand.
>
> Before getting back to work, she takes a moment to scroll through Instagram.
>
> Within 30 seconds, she's confronted by an ad that reads, "The Hub & Spoke Strategy: How one blog article per month can 20X your qualified leads."
>
> She thinks to herself, "That sounds pretty good. But what is The Hub & Spoke Strategy?"
>
> She clicks through to a landing page with a free eBook about The Hub & Spoke Strategy. The eBook isn't gated, meaning she doesn't have to enter her contact details to get it. She thinks to herself, that's a nice change. She downloads the eBook, spends about six minutes skimming through it, and is immediately impressed with the ideas.

She also notices how The Hub & Spoke Strategy is positioned as a very clear and direct offer. The pricing is right there on the page: $12,500 for a strategy plus two months of coaching.

She thinks to herself, "Why doesn't everyone make it this easy to understand what they're offering?" Impressed, she decides to do a little research on the company that put this out.

Upon finding their website, she's surprised to see that they're also a full-service marketing agency. They offer a range of services that align with what she's looking for. After almost a month of searching for a new Agency of Record, she wonders to herself, "Could this be the one?"

She reaches out through the contact page, books a meeting, interviews the team, and a few phone calls later, decides to hire them on a project basis to start.

Midway through the project, things are going well and she's learning more about the agency's philosophy and broader set of service offerings.

One month later she comes to a clear decision. She hires them as her new Agency of Record.

What a relief.

And so... as the sun began to set on a day well had, they all went skipping away together into the sunset, holding hands, eating ice cream and laughing ;)

What's the difference between these two experiences?

In the first experience, the client reviews the typical agency website that includes a vague positioning statement (We Deliver Big Ideas That Matter), a commonplace set of services, and a standard agency process.

In the second experience, the client reviews a productized **offer**, centered around a clear end result (20X your leads) with a unique mechanism to achieve that result (The Hub & Spoke Strategy). An offer that's being used as a hook to attract clients into a first meeting, before potentially converting them into AOR relationships.

In a study from The Corporate Executive Board Company (CEB), research indicates that B2B clients are 70% more likely to purchase a service where the seller has shown a clear model around how they can help their clients. The likelihood increases another 20% when the seller communicates a "specific and measurable result."

That combination of a clear end result, and a unique mechanism, can be productized, priced, and crafted into a strategic offer.

A topic we'll cover in the next chapter.

CHAPTER 13

THE STRATEGIC OFFER

Today, the best expertise providers understand how to craft a strategic offer, productize and price it, then use it as a hook to generate qualified sales meetings.

In the "Hub & Spoke Strategy" example shared previously, a full-service agency created a strategic offer around using content marketing to generate leads. This tactic was used to hook their dream clients into a conversation where they could then share the broader scope of what they do. Because ultimately, they were a full-service agency looking for AOR clients.

They productized an offer and used it as a hook.

But let's draw a quick distinction between a high-value strategic offer and snake oil.

We've all fallen victim to a great hook. We've been scrolling through Instagram and come across some online 'marketing guru' who speaks our language, promising some magic system that produces crazy results.

We then click through to purchase some book or online course, only to be disappointed with a bunch of crap we already knew.

Unfortunately, you'll always find these snake oil sellers who utilize similar principles to earn a quick buck. Who provide a false promise of value; one that turns out to be about as valuable as what you might extract from ChatGPT with a single well-crafted question.

Because a well-positioned offer works on just about anyone. It works on you. It works on me. And it works on your dream client.

The distinction lies in the value behind the offer. In your ability to actually produce results. Because by doing so, you'll be able to lead people deeper into your world where you can then expand and grow those accounts over time.

From Services to Offers

Every agency has a list of services they provide. But a list of services doesn't do much to get you new clients. This is where creating a great offer comes into play, which is a matter of productization and pricing.

There are entire books written around the structure of a great offer, and this isn't one of them. I'll therefore only provide a brief summary of what a great offer typically includes:

1. A clearly defined audience.
2. A clear end result you can achieve for that audience.
3. The unique mechanism you'll use to produce that result.
4. A clear (and potentially public) pricing model.

To provide context, a productized offer would typically exist on a landing page. You would run outbound marketing tactics to drive qualified traffic to that page with a call to action to book a meeting. That landing page would lay out the full offer, speaking to the clients' problems, your solution, and the results they can achieve. And, in some cases, the pricing would be presented right there on the page.

Transparent Pricing

I would never encourage you (or any agency) to publish their pricing publicly on their website. But in the case of a strategic offer (that lives on a separate landing page) I would encourage you to at least consider it. As a general rule of thumb, I encourage agencies to follow one simple rule:

Never hide your pricing from a prospective client.

Never think that if you hold back on sharing your pricing, the client will be more open to it later (after you've managed to impress them).

If you're on a first sales call and someone asks what the price range might be, you should be prepared to give them a quick answer. You should know your pricing and communicate it readily as a mechanism to weed out the timewasters.

The same thinking applies to a productized offer.

How many times have you landed on a website, looking to purchase a software solution for example, only to find that the pricing is not publicly available. They're forcing you to request a quote or book a demo - just to find the pricing. Aggravated, you leave the website and never look back. The truth is: people want to know how much things cost as quickly as possible.

A study by Nielsen Norman Group found that 20% of users abandon a website if they can't find the pricing information they're looking for. A separate study by ConversionXL found that companies who displayed pricing information on their websites experienced an average conversion rate increase of 21%.

Forcing a prospect to spend time meeting with you, just to determine how expensive you are, is a terrible idea. Why waste 30 minutes on an introductory call just to determine that the client can't afford you?

They can either afford you, or they can't afford you. It's really that simple. And if your approach is to convince them to spend more money than they can afford – shame on you. This only leads to a stressed relationship where the client is constantly worried about how much money they're spending, while expecting the world from you.

Not a situation you want to be in.

If the pricing model you share publicly scares away certain clients: mission accomplished. Because those who can't afford you should take a hike.

If you can master the art and science of creating a compelling productized offer, you'll create a pipeline of dream clients who understand what you're promising, know how much it costs, and with that information - still want to meet with you. Creating the most qualified new business meetings you could ever possibly have.

Pricing Architecture

Taking this one step further, I call it a pricing "model" because I also encourage you to implement pricing architecture when possible. More specifically, I recommend three tiers of pricing with most offers (or with most estimates in general).

For simplicity, let's call the three tiers of pricing low, medium and high. With each tier providing a different scope to deliver different value.

As one might expect, research has shown that customers typically choose the middle option. A phenomenon known as "the decoy effect" where the presence of other less attractive options help to steer an individual toward the most appealing option.

A study conducted by HubSpot found that companies providing three tiers of pricing had a 25% higher conversion rate than those with only two pricing options, and that two pricing options had a 10% higher conversion rate than those with only one.

A separate study conducted by UCLA found that providing multiple pricing options tends to increase the customers' perceived value of the product or service.

This brings us back to perceived value. A strategic offer is a great way to enhance your perceived value with your dream clients. It also becomes an incredibly powerful tool for lead generation and prospect qualification.

Creating an offer is the productization and pricing of what you do. Clients like this because it shows them you have a repeatable process – that must work – or why would you still be doing it?

A great offer is one where it would almost be illogical for the client to turn down a meeting because your offer is so specific to them, their problems, and the results they desire that – even if they already have an agency – it's still worth meeting you.

Next, we'll discuss what all this amounts to. A compelling story about how you can transform your client's business for the better.

CHAPTER 14

THE CLIENT TRANSFORMATION STORY™

Ever since there was language, there were stories.

Stories add emotion to thoughts and ideas. They influence how we relate to one another. How we pass ideas from person to person, culture to culture – and across generations.

They show us what's possible – sharing bits of the past to illuminate the future. They inspire dreams and provide hope, wielding the power to unite diverse groups around common goals.

So, what story should you be telling your dream clients?

It's a story about the journey you're going to take them on. A story about the transformation you'll help them achieve and how you're going to get there.

By now, I hope we're aligned on the following:

1. You need to clarify who your **dream client** is.
2. You need to clarify the **end results** you can produce for that client.
3. You need to clarify the **unique mechanisms** you'll use to to do so.
4. You can then craft those into **strategic offers** and use them to hook your dream clients into a first meeting.

These are the building blocks of a compelling story; what you bait your hook with before you cast it into the water. A juicy little story that will have your dream clients chomping at the bit.

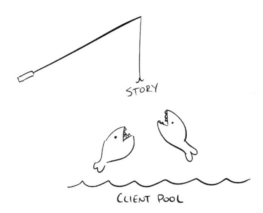

A Client Transformation Story™ (CTS) is a framework that describes how you will transform your client's business for the better.

It's a story you tell, a model you share, a picture you paint, to forge a connection with your dream clients. And there are two types of CTS:

1. An offer you use to engage prospects into a first meeting.
2. A philosophy you share to convert those opportunities into longer-term relationships.

The Project Offer CTS is what we covered in the previous chapter; a productized strategic offer used to hook your dream clients into that first meeting, which may lead to securing a short-term project engagement.

The AOR Philosophy CTS is a broader narrative used to convert existing conversations or projects into longer-term (AOR) relationships. It's typically a more robust story that shares your organizational philosophy, ties together your set of services, and demonstrates how you can help your clients holistically transform their businesses for the better (as opposed to the results they might achieve from a single project).

Remember The Hub & Spoke Strategy? That was a Project Offer CTS used by a full-service agency to get new clients in the door – before converting them into AOR clients.

EXAMPLE

Project Offer vs AOR Philosophy

Consulting Firm X specializes in corporate culture consulting. They offer both short-term project engagements as well as annual retainer contracts.

Depending on the opportunity, they use both a Project Offer CTS and an AOR Philosophy CTS.

Let's first review their [Project Offer CTS](#):

The 90-Day Engagement Boost

For HR Leaders Looking to Boost Engagement

As an HR leader, you dream of building an engaged and thriving culture. You look to other companies with admiration, seeing their social feeds filled with images of happy faces and engaged employees. All the while wondering - is that real? And how can we do that for our company?

With veiled frustration, you continue to read articles and watch videos, all the while struggling to figure out how you can repair your somewhat broken culture; how you can provide a better place to work for everyone involved.

In our 90-Day Engagement Boost program, we'll help you achieve a two-point boost to your employee engagement score within 90 days.

We implement our engagement tracking software, conduct a baseline survey, host leadership and employee workshops, develop and implement our systems and strategies, then measure again after 90 days.

Now let's review their <u>AOR Philosophy CTS</u> for an annual retainer contract.

THE 24/7 CULTURE PROGRAM

How the Best Organizations Put Culture First

Working to produce an organization-wide cultural shift is like standing at the foot of Mt. Everest, by yourself, wondering where to start.

Culture is evergreen... something you need to work on every day, every week, every month, for as long as you're in business. The world's most successful organizations tend to have one thing in common: a thriving and engaged workforce. And they get there by investing in their culture.

In our 24/7 Culture program, we'll assess your situation and build you a custom program around our four key pillars of Personal Leadership, Group Accountability, True Empowerment, and Fluid Communication.

To start, we implement our proprietary engagement tracking software, conduct baseline surveys, host leadership and employee workshops, then implement our systems and strategies. But, great cultures are a long-term investment.

Over time, we stay engaged, conducting quarterly meetings and workshops to iterate and enhance those systems and strategies year after year. This ensures a culture that continues to evolve, strengthen and thrive for years to come. Because all great cultures are 24/7.

In the above example, Consulting Firm X might use the Project Offer CTS to book new clients into a first meeting, where they would then ask questions to understand the client's business better. From there, they would determine whether to sell them on a short-term project engagement or a long-term retainer relationship. In which case, they would use the AOR Philosophy CTS as their narrative.

But for this to work, you need to be an excellent listener. In the words of a former client of mine, "There's a reason we have two ears, but only one mouth."

Listen to your potential clients, understand where they're at and what they need - then determine which story you should be telling them, and when.

Defining your client transformation stories will enable you to develop sales and marketing content that converts.

It's a paradigm shift from talking about your agency to talking about the client. It's the difference between sharing a list of services and telling a compelling story.

A story your dream client can see themselves in about a journey they want to embark on. A story that stokes their willingness to be led by someone who's demonstrating the expertise and leadership they've been looking for. A willingness to be led by someone who understands them.

PART 4

MARKET POSITIONING

The Layers of Market Positioning

Harpoons & Helicopters

Acquiring Objectivity

As we've now reached the halfway point of this book, let's take a moment to briefly recap what's been discussed so far.

I started by pointing out how most agencies are notoriously bad at taking proper care of themselves. How the first step toward building a scalable agency is treating yourself with the same level of care and strategic attention that you would your most important client.

This starts with a deep assessment of your core business model. To reconsider what you do, who you do it for, and how you can re-engineer your offerings to provide greater value to your dream clients.

Finally, we discussed how you can turn all that into strategic offers, and wrap them in compelling stories, about how you'll transform your client's business for the better.

Next, we'll discuss how to position all of this to the market.

Market Positioning *is the art and science of aligning your external touchpoints along an intentional customer journey.*

CHAPTER 15

THE LAYERS OF MARKET POSITIONING

Your market positioning can be seen as an interdependent set of layers. Starting at the base with your core business model. Then building onto that: how you communicate your business model through your narrative, how you present it through your digital presence, and how you go to market with your outreach.

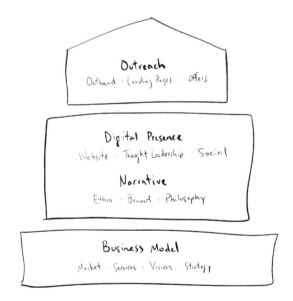

To build a high-performing customer journey, you must be highly intentional about the interplay between these layers. You must think through both the order in which they need to be developed, and the order in which they are ultimately consumed.

These layers can therefore be viewed from three different perspectives:

1. The order of development;
2. The order of consumption;
3. And as a continuum from fixed to variable positioning.

I will briefly explain each perspective.

Perspective 1: The Order of Development

These layers can only be developed in one logical order.

We start with a clearly defined business model.

- **Your Market:** Who You Serve.
- **Your Services:** What You Do.
- **Your Vision:** Where You're Going.
- **Your Strategy:** How You'll Get There.

You bring that business model to life through your brand narrative and digital presence. Through your website, thought leadership content and social channels.

Finally, you push it all out into the market through your outreach; whatever tactics you employ to generate new business meetings.

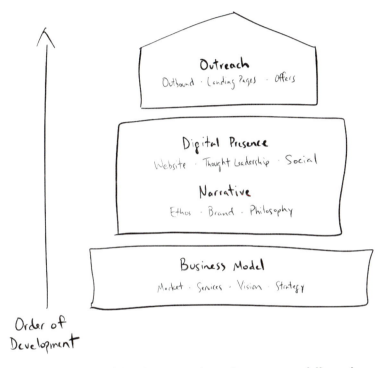

Order of Development

This is the order of development; the order you must follow when developing each layer of your market positioning.

Perspective 2: The Order of Consumption

Although these layers are developed from the ground up, they are consumed from the top down. Because the customer journey flows in the opposite direction.

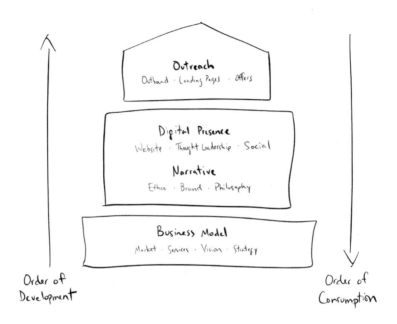

Your dream client is first hooked through your outreach.

Perhaps they receive an email, a LinkedIn message, or see an ad on social media and click through to a landing page that presents a strategic offer.

If the client is interested in your offer, they'll likely move into a brief online research phase to figure out who you are. They would dive deeper into your digital presence, view your website, peruse your thought leadership content and possibly check out your social channels. Consuming bits of your narrative at each step along this journey.

The average client does all of this before deciding to book a meeting. After which, they would enter your sales process, where you would meet to determine their needs, then pitch them accordingly.

And if you successfully bring them on as a new client, they'll step into your business model, where you'll work to produce whatever results were promised.

This is the order of consumption; the path a client follows through your intentional customer journey.

Perspective 3: Fixed vs Variable Positioning

The layers of market positioning also exist on a continuum from fixed to variable.

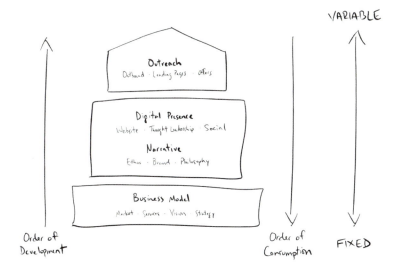

Your business model is the most fixed of these layers, as it should remain relatively solid and unchanged over long-term periods of three to five years. Your narrative is similar, but more flexible than the business model itself.

As we get into your digital presence, there's far more wiggle room to experiment and revise each year – or even each month.

While at the most variable end of this continuum, your outreach can come and go like the wind; a playground where you test different strategies to see what works.

At the fixed end of this continuum, you have things that are harder to change; that have a more significant impact on the business.

At the variable end of this continuum, you have things that are easier to change; that have a less significant impact on the business.

If I were to paraphrase what I do with my clients into its simplest form, it would be pushing them to rethink their layers of market positioning. An extremely complex task that involves rethinking everything from who your dream client is to what your business model delivers to how you position your brand, digital presence and offers. Plus, the tactics you'll use to pull dream clients into and through your customer journey.

Understanding and becoming intentional about the layers of market positioning is a crucial step toward developing a high-performing new business program.

Many agencies, at first glance, would look at these layers, proclaim them to be obvious, then state that they're already doing all of this. I'm then left with the awkward task of gingerly pointing out that they're not really doing any of it properly.

Yes, you have a business model, narrative, digital presence and you do some outreach. But do these things work together as a high-performing customer journey? Does it spit out qualified meetings on a weekly basis? And are you able to consistently convert those meetings into clients each quarter?

The real answers to these questions often fail to become evident until they're looked at in concert with each other. Or, when put under the microscope of an objective outside observer.

CHAPTER 16

HARPOONS & HELICOPTERS

In this chapter, I'll provide a whale-hunting analogy that gives us another way to understand the layers of market positioning in action. Please note that I do not condone whale hunting :)

THAT DAY IN OCTOBER

The sky darkened as an ominous cluster of clouds grew closer. Although the weather forecast had predicted a calm and beautiful day – it was clearly taking a turn for the worse.

Perhaps it wasn't the best day for a whale hunt, but the ship had already set sail. Brutis and his crew looked over their shoulders, watching the coastline fade into oblivion as they thought to themselves, "There's no turning back now."

It was their third whale hunt this month, and they needed to make quota. At least this time, a glimmer of optimism graced their endeavors, for they had new information as to where a large group of whales might be congregating.

In the previous two hunts, they had relied purely on sonar to seek out the whales – with little success. But this time, they decided to pony up and hire a helicopter.

If they could locate a group of whales on sonar, they'd radio the chopper to come land on their ship deck, pick up a spotter, and take them up to 10,000 feet to gain a birds-

> eye view of the ship and its surrounding waters. A process whalers use to more effectively find and catch whales.
>
> They had also invested in some sharper and longer-range harpoon gear. It was time for these investments to pay off. This would be the hunt where we finally bag a few big ones!

Whale hunting is a difficult and resource-intensive task.

A modern whale-hunting operation not only requires a solid ship. You also need a set of high quality harpoons to hook and catch the whales. And a helipad on your ship deck, where helicopters can occasionally land to take you up for a bird's eye view. This chapter is about the two things most agencies lack: harpoons and helicopters.

Every agency has a ship.

It's what you ride into the rough waters of agency competition.

The ship represents the more fixed elements of your market positioning: your core business model, narrative and digital presence.

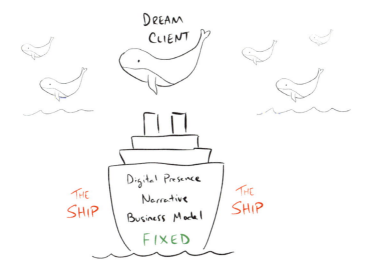

But a ship alone won't do much to catch whales.

Just as having an agency doesn't mean you'll get clients.

You'll need some high-quality harpoons.

Harpoons enable you to effectively hook and catch the whales, before you bring them aboard your ship. Those harpoons represent your outreach. They represent the most variable component of your market positioning - the outbound marketing tactics and productized offers you shoot into the world to hook your dream clients.

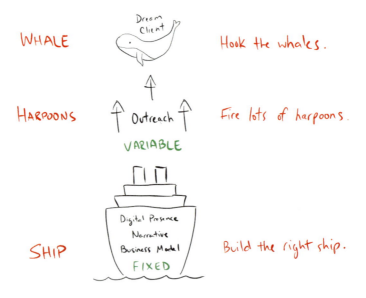

If you fire one and miss – not a big deal.

Just load up another – and shoot again.

You can do this by modifying the offer itself or the landing page it lives on. You can also switch the outbound marketing tactics you're using to drive traffic.

Just switch it out, load it up, and fire another harpoon.

> *"You miss 100% of the shots you don't take."*
> Wayne Gretzky

Simply put: most agencies just aren't taking enough shots. They aren't loading up enough harpoons or firing them often enough.

Each harpoon you fire represents a productized offer. It's how you hook and pull dream clients onto your ship (where you can then metaphorically harvest their blubber ;)

Because once aboard your ship, you can introduce them to your broader philosophy (where you might inspire them to stick around for the long-term).

Shit... maybe you can even get them to swab the deck!

Just remember that your harpoons are attached to very thick ropes. Each time you fire one, you can reel it back in, then fire it again. The more harpoons you fire, the more whales you're going to catch.

It's really that simple.

Finally, you'll need a helipad on your ship deck.

As the captain, it's your responsibility to steer the ship. You stand, with your feet firmly planted on the ship deck. Looking out from a vantage point that offers a limited view. You can't possibly see the entire ship, or its surrounding waters, from where you stand.

Thus, every so often, you need that helicopter to pull you up off the ship deck, where you can gain an entirely different perspective.

The helipad represents your willingness to seek objective outside counsel. Your willingness to ensure that your business decisions are sound.

This comes in the form of an advisory board, outside consultant or through the practice of customer inclusion.

Because the truth is – you (the business owner) will have a hard time being objective when looking at your own business.

You're too deep in your own environment.

True objectivity is something you can only acquire externally.

In summary, start by getting your ship in order. A solid business model, brand narrative and digital presence. Then use harpoons as a testing ground. Create and launch productized offers until you learn what works.

And every so often, be wise enough to radio the chopper.

CHAPTER 17

ACQUIRING OBJECTIVITY

There's an Ethiopian proverb that goes:

"Fish discover water last."

Fish don't have the awareness that water even exists until the first time they're pulled out of that environment. Out of the water they're immersed in.

Human beings are similar. We become so immersed in our day-to-day environments that it becomes difficult for us to see them as they truly are, just as the fish don't see the water.

Similar to how you can't see your entire ship while you're standing on the ship deck.

Never fool yourself into thinking you have a special ability to look at your own business objectively. Very few people do, myself included.

I once led the strategic repositioning of a $6 billion dollar company with 6,300 employees across 42 countries. It took nine months and involved leading executive workshops in 11 different countries across five continents. The project was a huge success, winning global marketing campaign of the year at a prestigious awards gala in the United Kingdom.

Yet, I recently attempted to reposition my own consulting practice, which saw me spend six months spinning in circles, changing my mind constantly, before finally deciding to take my own advice and seek outside help.

Six weeks later, I had a perfectly repositioned consulting practice.

Not only was I unable to reposition myself effectively, despite being a repositioning expert. I also wasn't smart enough to take my own advice. To practice what I preach.

Which, by the way, is the core premise of this book. I failed to treat myself with the same level of care and attention that I would my most important client.

I failed to treat myself like a client.

Simply put: don't be dumb like I was. Keep your helipad ready and know when it's time to radio the chopper.

PART 5

SYSTEMIZING REPEATABLE GROWTH

Aspirational Positioning

Growth Modelling

Reverse Engineered Metrics

The "In-House" Client Model

SYSTEMIZING REPEATABLE GROWTH

HERE'S THE LOGIC

You likely aspire to one day sell your agency for as much money as possible. You therefore want to create a sellable agency – with a high valuation.

To do this, you must demonstrate consistent and impressive revenue growth, across multiple years, with a healthy profit margin. And there are three mechanisms required to make this work:

1. **Value Enhancement:** You must consistently re-engineer your services to fight commoditization and deliver greater value to your dream clients, then better productize and package those services, so you can charge higher prices and earn higher margins.

2. **Steady Acquisition:** You must systemize a client acquisition model that consistently delivers qualified meetings and converts those meetings into clients.

3. **Margin Shift:** You must add new high-profit clients while finding the courage to slowly shed the low-profit clients and services that erode your profit margins.

Every concept in this book is designed to support the above three mechanisms.

So, if you are (indeed) working toward building a sellable high-value agency, what should your annual goals look like along the way?

You should aspire to the gold standard of consistently achieving 20%+ year-over-year growth with a 20% net profit margin.

A difficult task that requires a mindset shift from landing the odd big client here or there to consistently landing high value clients, quarter after quarter, on repeat. Something that is only achievable after you've developed the proper systems.

And I do mean **systems**. Not some loosely strung-together set of marketing tactics, that you occasionally execute when you can find the time, leading prospects into a 'fly-by-the-seat-of-your-pants' sales process that reinvents itself with each new sales opportunity.

The systemization of repeatable and profitable growth requires you to become far more intentional in your approach.

In the next set of chapters, we'll discuss how to set intentional and ambitious goals, develop accurate sales forecasts, reverse engineer those forecasts to create an effective marketing strategy – then arrange your people around achieving that strategy.

CHAPTER 18
ASPIRATIONAL POSITIONING

"Dress for the job you want, not the job you have."

Austin Kleon

My first 'real job' was as an Account Coordinator at McKim Cringan George; the first (ever) ad agency in Canada (founded in 1889).

During my second week on the job, I was invited to my first client meeting. I was told to come, but to only listen and observe. Not to participate.

"Whatever you do, just don't say anything," I was told.

As we prepared to leave, I met the rest of the team in the lobby near the elevators. I was the first one there. The last person to show up was one of the VPs who walked up, looked me up and down, and asked, "Is that what you're wearing?"

In an instant, I felt every muscle in my body tighten; I was mortified. It was as if my feet were suddenly cemented into the floor. I looked down at my clothing and wondered, what's wrong with what I'm wearing? I had on black slacks, light brown dress shoes and a tucked in, patterned dress shirt.

As the elevator doors opened, and the group began to board the elevator, I struggled to unfreeze my feet, barely making it through the doors in time.

I was mentally and emotionally ruined for the rest of that day.

When I got home that evening, without even taking my shoes off, I proceeded to stand in front of the mirror, staring at myself for about 20 minutes. Coming to the realization that I looked like a child who was wearing his father's clothing.

My embarrassment grew stronger. Was this an accurate observation? Or was my judgement clouded by a bruised ego?

Did it really matter?

I took a pee, ate a mandarin orange, then immediately drove to the mall where I proceeded to buy an entirely new work wardrobe. Never again would I be seen this way.

It wasn't long after this experience when I first heard that quote:

"Dress for the job you want, not the job you have."

Although I'd just went through a very literal iteration of this quote, I immediately understood it's broader metaphorical significance. It's a quote about how you should position yourself to the world. And nowhere could this quote be more relevant than in how you position your company to the world.

You should be positioning yourself for the clients you want, not the clients you have.

Aspirational positioning is about looking five years into the future, understanding what you want to become, then making it so – by positioning yourself as such – today.

It's about embedding a stretch goal, directly into your brand, that will immediately apply the pressure to move forward, and the motivation to evolve.

It's like placing a big new pair of shoes in front of yourself – then stepping into them. At first, these new shoes don't fit. They're too big and you'll have to grow into them.

But, when the day comes where these new shoes fit perfectly, you'll know it's time to look another five years into the future. To put the next pair of new shoes in front of yourself and step into them with confidence.

Aspirational positioning gives you something to live up to; something to work towards. Because, when you proclaim your aspirational positioning to the world, you immediately create the pressure to make it real.

I'll provide a simplified example.

> A fictional agency called Williams Martin has the following brand positioning statement:
>
> *We help aerospace companies solve marketing problems.*
>
> Although I might applaud how specialized they are in their positioning, it could certainly be more aspirational. For example, they could instead say:

> *The world's leading aerospace marketing agency.*
>
> Now, the first question is – are they the world's leading aerospace marketing agency? Or more importantly, is there another agency that can claim this throne?
>
> Probably not. Therefore, that spot is open for the taking.
>
> They can make that visionary, aspirational claim. They can plant that flag in the ground and be honest about it being aspirational. That it's the vision they're working towards.
>
> They can say to their clients, "Our goal is to be the world's leading aerospace marketing agency and it's right there on the header of our homepage. That's what we're all about, and we wear it proudly."
>
> It doesn't matter if they're currently the world's leading aerospace marketing agency. What matters is that they're telling everyone that their primary goal is to be the world's leading aerospace marketing agency. Clients will appreciate that ambition as well as the clarity of their vision.

Aspirational positioning is a unique form of (indirect) goal-setting. By embedding a stretch goal directly into your core brand positioning, it lights a fire under the agency.

It forces your people to step into that big new pair of shoes and to grow into the next iteration of what your agency needs to become.

CHAPTER 19

GROWTH MODELLING

"If you can look into the seeds of time, and say which grain will grow and which will not, speak then unto me."

William Shakespeare

Not all agencies develop growth forecasts for their YOY growth. And for those who do, their forecasts often lack enough detail to be useful in guiding their sales and marketing activities.

These forecasts are often based on little to no science, taking growth from the last couple years and simply extending that trend forward into the future.

When I ask executive leaders what their financial goals are, I'm often given suspiciously round numbers such as "$20 million in five years" or "15% YOY growth."

I then discover that the extent of their growth forecasting comes down to a single tab in a spreadsheet that shows total revenue going up "a little bit" each year with no detail around **how** that will happen or where it will come from.

How does one execute against that?

I suppose the strategy would be to land as much new business as possible, then see how close you come to your goals. Let's call it a "hope for the best" strategy. Similar to the "take what we can get" approach mentioned earlier.

If this sounds familiar, you're not alone. This is pretty much the norm in most agencies.

I expect this is likely because most agencies are founded by 'creative types' who aren't particularly interested in learning about or understanding 'the numbers.' These creative types will learn the bare minimum required to run a business and hate every second of it. Hoping to instead spend their time coming up with 'big ideas' or 'making cool stuff.'

I understand this because it describes me perfectly. I'm also the 'creative type' who hates 'the numbers' and prefers to spend my time 'making cool stuff.'

I love making cool stuff.

But, as I'm sure you know, the numbers are incredibly important. And proper growth forecasting is an essential component in setting yourself up to scale.

So fair warning, this section may not be as much fun to read. It may be harder to follow. But the topics discussed are essential to your growth strategy.

Growth Modelling

How does one forecast top-line revenue growth in a way that isn't just extending the trend forward from previous years or making up numbers out of thin air?

We do this through a process called growth modelling.

Growth Modelling is the detailed mapping of what we want to see happen in the coming year. Not only how much revenue growth we want to achieve, but when we will achieve it and where it will come from. It's where we answer the questions: what will we sell, who will we sell it to, and when?

I'll draw a quick comparison to bring this concept into focus.

An audience persona is a semi-fictional representation of your ideal audience. This is Nancy, your ideal client. She does this, she does that, here is why, etc.

A growth model is a semi-fictional representation of your ideal year. We will land 3 AOR clients and 7 projects. Here are specific dollar amounts for each. Here is when we will land each of them. Here are the industries, company types and services we will provide for each.

The process of imagining your ideal year, in this level of detail, can quickly illuminate whether or not your goals are realistic. Perhaps your goals are too big. Perhaps your goals are too small.

It forces you to take a hard look at what would be required to achieve different revenue targets. The number of clients you would have to land, the size of each account, and how frequently you would have to land them.

Client	Amount	Close Date	Start Date	Revenue Stream			
				Jan	Feb	Mar	Apr...
Coca Cola	$350K	Jan	Mar			$20K	$30K
Ferrari	$450K	Jan	Jan	$70K	$30K	$30K	$30K
Etc.	—	—	—	—	—	—	—

This then informs the how. What you would have to do, from a marketing perspective, to make this happen. And that understanding provides a runway to reverse engineer the metrics you'll use to design your marketing program.

CHAPTER 20

REVERSE ENGINEERED METRICS

Reverse engineering your marketing metrics is the process of working backwards from your annual sales targets to determine what needs to be accomplished in your marketing.

To fully understand the reverse engineering of your marketing metrics, we must first acknowledge how accountability flows through the organization.

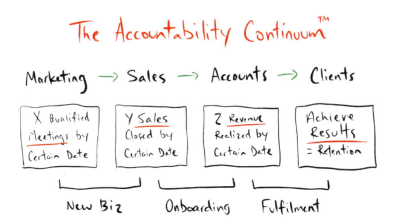

To achieve your new business revenue targets, you'll need to generate a certain number of leads, convert a percentage of those leads into meetings, convert a percentage of those meetings into proposals, turn a percentage of those proposals into new clients, onboard those clients successfully, hand them over to your accounts team, execute the work effectively, keep the client happy, complete any projects, produce results for the client, collect payment - and do so all within a specified time frame to achieve your revenue targets.

That string of dependencies should be understood and mapped. And with that understanding in place, we can reverse engineer each step in this process to establish metrics that will show us exactly what needs to happen if we are to achieve our goals.

This is best illustrated through a detailed example:

> Agency X offers brand development services.
>
> They build a growth model and determine that next year's new business revenue target will be $200,000. Consisting of four $50,000 branding engagements (one per quarter throughout the year).
>
> It typically takes 5 qualified new business meetings to find 1 client who wants to receive a proposal with pricing. And based on past proposal history, they typically close on 1 out of 3 proposals. Therefore, they need 15 qualified meetings to close one $50,000 deal.
>
> **15 meetings = 3 proposals = 1 x $50,000 deal**
>
> This means they need 60 qualified meetings to achieve their annual new business target of $200,000.
>
> **60 meetings = 12 proposals = 4 x $50,000 deals = $200,000**

Let's pause here for a moment. I first want to point out that the primary goal of your marketing efforts should be to generate qualified new business meetings. Understanding how many qualified meetings are required to achieve your annual growth target is an incredibly powerful metric – and first step – to building an effective marketing program.

> Agency X has determined they need 60 qualified meetings per year, which is 15 meetings per quarter, 5 meetings per month or 1.25 meetings per week.
>
> This leads us to the next logical question: what is required to generate 60 qualified new business meetings?
>
> Again, from historical data, Agency X knows that it typically takes 20 clicks from a marketing email through to a landing page to get one meeting booked. And knowing that visitors have seen the offer (with pricing) and still want to meet with you is what qualifies them. Therefore, the math is as follows:
>
> To generate one $50,000 sale, they must send 3 proposals, which requires 15 meetings, which requires 300 clicks.
>
> **300 clicks = 15 meetings = 3 proposals = 1 x $50,000 deal**
>
> Therefore, to meet their $200,000 sales target, they must send 12 proposals, which requires 60 meetings, which requires 1200 clicks.
>
> **1200 clicks = 60 meetings = 12 proposals =**
> **4 x $50,000 deals = $200,000**

> That 1200 clicks also needs to be spread out evenly throughout the year, converting to a metric of 100 clicks per month (or 23 clicks per week).
>
> So the next step is determining how to achieve 100 clicks per month.

And that's where you marketing strategy comes into play.

You can then build your strategy around one simple goal: 100 clicks per month. Which enables you to better focus your efforts.

$$\underline{100 \text{ clicks}/\text{month}} = \underline{\text{success}}$$

That's also where my example ends.

It's on you to determine what tactics will work best with your specific audience. Whether it's cold email outreach, LinkedIn direct messaging, old school methods like physical direct mail, blasting attendees at a relevant conference and so on.

But assuming you've done everything else in this book to get your business and your offers positioned properly, this is where the magic starts to happen. Where you start to achieve results beyond your wildest dreams – simply because you know what results you're trying to achieve, and you can be intentional about how you're going to achieve them.

To do this, you'll need historical data such as your opportunity close rates, lead-to-meeting conversion rates, and more. And if you don't currently keep track of these metrics, you need to start doing so immediately.

And for those who don't have those metrics, you can use the ratios provided in the above example as a starting point. You can also use Google or ChatGPT to search relevant industry averages.

Armed with reverse engineered marketing metrics, you can develop a thoughtful and precise marketing plan. You can determine how many people you need to reach, how many campaigns it will require, and when to launch them.

This is how the world's best marketers build their marketing plans.

> *"An unsophisticated forecaster uses statistics as a drunken man uses lampposts – for support rather than illumination."*
> Andrew Lang, Novelist

Next, we'll discuss the level of intentionality required to put all of this into action across your teams, systems and culture.

How to treat yourself like a client.

CHAPTER 21

THE "IN-HOUSE" CLIENT MODEL

To achieve any of what's been discussed in this book so far, there's one underlying principle that rules them all.

You'll need to become your single most important client.

Treating yourself like a client is a good start, but what I'm saying goes beyond that. You need to put yourself first, ahead of all other clients. To put your own mask on, before assisting others. In this chapter, we'll discuss what that looks like from an operational standpoint.

The "In-House" Client

It starts by establishing an internal team that will be held accountable to achieving your new business revenue targets. This team is responsible for growth modelling, goal setting, building your marketing plan, overseeing its execution, managing sales opportunities, and securing new business accounts.

At a minimum, this team would typically include the agency principal, a salesperson if you have one, a marketing person if you have one, and whoever manages your accounting (so you can keep track of the numbers in real-time, as you go).

This team becomes the client. We'll refer to them as the "in-house client." The in-house client then uses the rest of the agency, as any other client would.

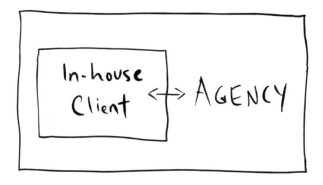

Your Dedicated Agency Team

You'll also need a dedicated agency team. Depending on the size of your agency and the skillsets you have in-house, this could include a lead designer, web dev lead, digital marketing lead, and so on.

The idea here is to assign a consistent team that will handle all creative development to support the execution of your sales and marketing activities. By using a consistent and dedicated team, as you would with any other client, they'll understand your needs better over time, thereby producing better results as you go.

You should also assign an account coordinator to manage projects and keep everything on track - because the devil is in the details.

You must learn to treat yourself with the same level of effort, detail, and professionalism as you would your most important client. You can't just "play client" until things get busy, then push yourself to the side in place of "real client work." Because the thing is: you're not just any other client.

You're the single most important client you'll ever have.

BECOMING YOUR 'LARGEST' CLIENT

You not only want to become your most important client. You also want to become your largest client (by way of revenue generated).

I'll use some slightly sketchy math to make my point.

The new business revenue generated each year, by your in-house client, should exceed the revenue generated by any other single client.

This would be easy to achieve with project work, so let's consider this in the context of AOR clients.

Let's say you did $3M in annual revenue last year. Then grew by 10%, thereby generating $300K in new business revenue.

Let's also say that your largest client does $1M per year. This means your new business revenue fails to exceed the revenue generated by your largest external client (because $300K is less than $1M).

Furthermore, this means your new business program is likely underperforming and you're not on a path to scale.

However, this is normal. Many agencies have this problem.

Let's say you then reposition your agency and manage to land two $750K clients next year, totalling $1.5M in new business revenue generated.

And just like that you've become your own largest client. Because your new business revenue ($1.5M) exceeds that of your single largest client ($1M).

Then, as you continue to grow, you'll look to land larger and larger clients. Next you might land a $1.5M account, then a $2M account and so on.

This means you're on a path to scale. Your in-house client is generating more than any one external client - and you've now become your own largest client.

But this requires a leap of faith. Because you can't become your own largest client - until you've learned to treat yourself as your most important client. And done so for at least one year, because it takes time.

You must first learn to treat yourself like a client. You then become your most important client. Then finally, through persistence, you become your own largest client (by way of revenue generated).

And once that happens, I promise you'll never go back.

The in-house client model is comparable to how some clients choose to build in-house agencies.

But you're not some client building a *lackluster* in-house agency. **You're the agency that's building a powerful in-house client.** An interesting juxtaposition – and the precise thing that makes this model so tricky to execute; the fact that all of you work at the same company.

When things get crazy busy, you can't let the in-house client take a back seat to your other clients. Because as soon as you do this once, the whole system will begin to crumble. You'll return to your old ways, and to achieving your old results.

You'll have demonstrated to your team that the system is flexible. That you're not actually your most important client. And they will follow suit.

> *"Every system is perfectly designed to get the results that it does."*
>
> W. Edwards Deming

Treating yourself like a client isn't a theoretical concept. It's a practical method; an operational structure; and a requirement when looking to scale.

In the next set of chapters, we'll shift our discussion from operations to culture. Discussing how you can launch your new program internally by setting a clear destination, then getting everyone pulling in the same direction.

PART 6

CULTURAL SOCIALIZATION

Sum of the Vectors

Leaders Create Tension

The Big Announcement

CULTURE

[kul-chur] the shared values, beliefs and behaviors of a particular group within society.

SOCIALIZE

[so-shul-ize] to treat as a group activity.

To effectively start treating yourself like a client, the concept must be deeply socialized into your people, your teams, and your culture.

For this to become a high-performing system that produces repeatable results over time, it can't be a one-off, flash-in-the-pan moment where you briefly decide to invest in yourself, only to eventually slip back into your old ways. This new approach must be embedded into your everyday reality – by including everyone in the organization.

By getting everyone pulling in the same direction.

CHAPTER 22

SUM OF THE VECTORS

Many years ago, I attended the HubSpot Inbound Marketing Conference in Boston with a few colleagues. One of the largest marketing events in the world, bringing together over 21,000 marketing experts from around the globe.

During a keynote speech, one of HubSpot's co-founders (Dharmesh Shah) told a story about having breakfast with Elon Musk. He asked Elon, "You know Elon, you run five companies, have eight children, and are wildly successful. How do you keep it all together?"

Elon, who was taking a sip of his orange juice at the time, pulled the glass from his lips and (without a moment's hesitation) responded, "Sum of the vectors," before casually taking another sip.

Dharmesh sat there for a moment, dumbfounded by the response itself, as well as how quickly and casually Elon had provided it, before repeating back, "Sum of the vectors?"

Elon went on to explain that a vector is a combination of direction and velocity.

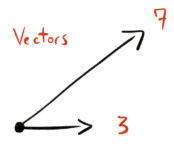

Let's say you draw a single point on a piece of paper. Then draw two lines coming out of this point. One is going up and to the right at a velocity of 7, while the other is going straight to the right at a velocity of 3.

If you add these two together, what velocity would you get?

While most people would say 10, the real answer is 4.

This is because the two vectors are going in two slightly different directions. This means they subtract from each other's velocity, unless they're both going in the exact same direction. Even a slight variation in trajectory results in a subtraction from the shared velocity.

The same is true of organizations. If you can't get everyone pulling in the same exact direction, then your people are subtracting from the shared velocity of the organization.

In most organizations, people have different agendas, objectives, and so on. Those differences cause people to pull in different directions, thereby slowing down the overall progress made.

To get everyone pulling in the same direction, you'll need to get everyone engaged around a clear destination. And it's the leader's role to set that clear destination, then shout it from the mountaintop – repeatedly.

CHAPTER 23

LEADERS CREATE TENSION

Imagine your organization as a group of people standing together holding one end of a bungee cord, while the leader stands beside them holding the other end of that bungee cord.

When the leader communicates an ambitious vision for the future, or sets stretch goals, the leader is effectively walking out ahead of the group until there's tension on the bungee cord.

As the leader, it's your duty to communicate those stretch goals, thereby creating that tension on the cord. Tension that will naturally pull everyone toward you – and the intended future you've placed in front of them.

But it's a fine line. If you pull too far ahead, you create too much tension on the cord, and the cord might snap. In that situation, your goals are too aggressive. People lose belief in what you're doing, become overworked, demotivated, and may choose to leave the organization.

But when you create just the right amount of tension – you can pull your people forward to the promised land.

Sum of the vectors ;)

Earlier, I wrote about Aspirational Positioning; about positioning yourself externally based on a vision of what you want to become in the future, rather than what you are today. This is a mechanism to create that tension on the cord. To get everyone pulling in the same direction. Tension that can only be released when the organization moves closer to achieving it's goals. To becoming what it was meant to be.

And when that tension is released, the leader must step forward again to create new tension - by communicating a new destination for the future.

CHAPTER 24

THE BIG ANNOUNCEMENT

After working through your strategic transformation, you'll reach that magic moment when it's time to hit the GO button. To shout your destination from the mountaintop. To create tension on the cord. To place that big new pair of shoes in front of everyone – and collectively step into them.

Bring the entire agency together for a big announcement. If you can do it in person, have some champagne ready on a table, with flutes lined up in neat little rows.

"We have a big announcement to make," you'll begin. "A new client that's gonna change everything…"

The anticipation will build as everyone starts to look around, wondering who it could be and how they haven't heard about this yet.

"This amazing new client… is us."

Your people, standing there on the verge of applause, will instead fall dead silent. Hands will return to people's sides as they turn to look at each other, confused.

"Wait a second… what?" someone will say out loud.

It'll be a strange, anti-climactic moment, no doubt.

But you'll then continue to explain, "I know it sounds strange but we're going to walk you through a brief presentation to explain what we're talking about, because this is a really big deal for us."

You can then walk your people through a 30-minute presentation that explains all the work you've done. Your new vision, your stretch goals, and any changes to your business model, positioning or strategy. You'll also explain how the new system is going to work; how you're going to start **treating yourself like an actual client.**

By the end of the presentation, your people will no longer look confused. They'll instead be excited about the clear new vision you've placed in front of them. About the big new pair of shoes you're about to step into. About the system you'll use to get there. And how everyone will be a part of making it happen.

Broad Inclusion

For this to work, everyone must feel included.

Your in-house client and agency teams shouldn't feel like elite groups that everyone else has been left out of. A simple approach to including others is to select people at random and have them sit in on strategy meetings or brainstorms. This gives everyone the opportunity to participate and contribute from time to time.

Not only does this serve to create an inclusive environment, but you might be surprised by the ideas that come from all corners of the organization.

Shared Accountability

You'll also need to install accountability systems to ensure results. I'll propose two methods.

The first method is regular internal communications about in-house client performance. Distribute a monthly or quarterly report to the entire organization that shares the goals for that time period versus the results you were able to achieve. But make it interesting. Include stories about the opportunities you had, what you pitched and how it went. Entertain people, let them see behind the veil, but also clearly communicate the goals you've set versus how you've performed.

It's remarkable what this does; when people know their work is not only being measured against clear goals, but reported publicly to the entire organization, people will step up their performance because they want to get credit for the work they've done.

The second method relates to your bonus structure. Some agencies provide bonuses to certain individuals or departments based on individual or team performance. I recommend you create one bonus structure for the entire organization that depends on overall revenue performance (and therefore, on new business performance). This will incentivize everyone to place new business on a pedestal. Causing everyone to actively contribute; to look for ways they can assist with your growth efforts, while ensuring you continue to treat yourself as your own most important client.

Designing a great system is one thing, but how you roll it out is just as important. How you socialize it into your culture and your operations.

Simply put – don't fumble on the five-yard line.

You can design the best system ever, but if you don't get your people on board – it will fail.

PART 7

COURAGE & COMMITMENT

Your Investment Strategy

The Emotional Cycles of Change

The final section of this book focuses purely on you, the leader. On your thoughts, feelings, and motivations as you work through this process. One could argue this is the most important part – finding the courage to invest in yourself, the guts to commit valuable resources, and the resilience to stay the course.

Because nothing happens overnight.

There's no quick, magical solution to scaling your agency.

The appropriate mindset is one of buckling in for a sustainable, long-term transformation.

CHAPTER 25
YOUR INVESTMENT STRATEGY

"The only investment that never fails is investing in yourself."

Warren Buffet

From becoming a more intentional leader, to becoming your own most important client, we can boil this book down to one simple concept: investing in yourself.

An investment that carries the potential to change your life, and your business, forever - if done properly. With that in mind, I'll share a few principles to guide your investment strategy.

1. Stop Thinking You Have Time.
2. Invest When Things are Good.
3. Step Away from Incrementalism.
4. Acquire Objectivity.

PRINCIPLE 1: Stop Thinking You Have Time

Why do 78% of agencies fail within the first 10 years?

Agencies must evolve as they grow. The world's fastest-growing and longest-lasting agencies have one thing in common: they appropriately understood the need to evolve their core business models at key points along their journey to growth. They understood the difference between doing $1M in annual revenue vs $2M vs $5M vs $10M and so on.

Over time, I believe the agency principal develops a warped perception of time, due to the unique stresses of agency life. Within the intense and relentless hustle and bustle, the years fly by - while the agency principal remains trapped, dancing on a line between driving new business and staying closely involved in major client relationships.

Within this juggling act, the mentality of self-investment is often an idea reserved for the future. And although this future is always right around the corner – it also never comes.

Such an investment is seen as having the time (and financial freedom) to sit down with your team, map out a new future, and reinvent where necessary. Something you're planning to do… eventually.

An upcoming process that lives on a perpetual horizon; something you can only start after you get over that "next hump."

That "next hump" might be landing another big client or finishing an important client project. A mirage in the distance that can never be reached. Because the moment you get over that "next hump" another hump appears right before your eyes. Over and over again, in an endless cycle.

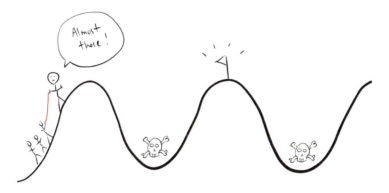

This idea of getting over that "next hump" is one I consistently hear from the agencies I speak with. They're doing reasonably well at the time, while looking for that next level of growth.

Yet, they're not quite ready to invest in themselves – referencing some goal in the future they need to achieve first. Then, a few months later, I receive a very different phone call. Something has changed and they've gone from doing reasonably well - into red alert mode.

The appropriate time to invest has passed and they're now fighting to stay above water.

> *"Our biggest problem is that we think we have time."*
> Buddha

PRINCIPLE 2: Invest When Things Are Good

The best time to invest is when things are going well. When you have the money to do so. When you have the confidence to do so. And preferably, when you have the time to do so (although that part isn't mandatory because you may never really "have" the time).

I often speak with agency principals who don't come right out and say it, but they're already in red alert mode. Contacting me as a last-ditch effort to save a failing business. Suddenly looking to invest - although they're likely taking on debt, in an effort to save the business, as opposed to using their own cash, in an effort to scale the business. Hardly what I could call an investment.

My point is this: you should invest when things are good. When things are looking up. When you have some flexibility around your time and money. Take advantage of the situation, invest in your future and build a system to scale.

Do it when you want to, not when you need to.

When you're on the mountaintop and things are going well, radio the chopper, pull yourself up for a birds-eye-view, and take some time to think through what's next.

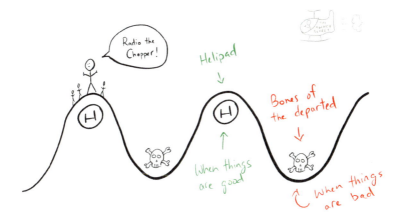

PRINCIPLE 3: Step Away from Incrementalism

Earlier in the book, we discussed incrementalism. The approach most companies take when looking to evolve. An approach that sees you tackling problems one by one, year after year, in a somewhat illogical order, based on immediate priority only. An approach that leaves you running on a hamster wheel to nowhere town.

At some point, you need to step off the hamster wheel. Assess your entire business. Map the holistic change your agency needs. Then execute that change within a single fiscal year. And look to repeat that process once every three to five years, having it become faster and easier each time.

It's the difference between taking the stairs or taking the elevator.

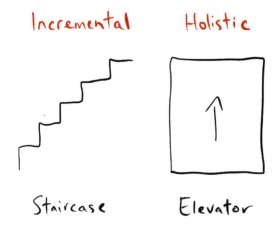

Incremental change is a staircase. Holistic change is an elevator.

I'm suggesting you take the elevator.

PRINCIPLE 4: Acquire Objectivity

Elevators are great, but helicopters are even better :)

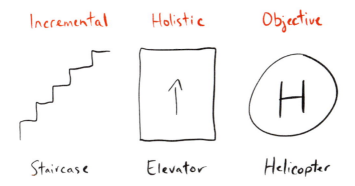

If the staircase represents incremental change, and the elevator represents holistic change... the helicopter represents something you can't achieve from anywhere inside the building.

It represents the capacity to be pulled up out of your business where you can gain an entirely new perspective on the building itself – and its surrounding environment.

The helicopter represents your willingness to seek objective, outside counsel. One of the wisest things you can ever do as a leader.

In Summary

Never let yourself believe that you have all the time in the world to get your shit together. Invest when things are going well. Acknowledge the need for broader change and don't tackle those changes in incremental bits over multiple years. Map your holistic transformation, then commit to executing it within a single year.

Have the courage to invest in yourself. To seek outside counsel. To do it once and do it right. And across all of this, remember to treat yourself as your single most important client.

CHAPTER 26

THE EMOTIONAL CYCLES OF CHANGE

I'll conclude this book with a story about the inherent weight, and emotional challenges, that come with running a business.

Years ago, I went through a rough patch. It was one of the more challenging and stressful periods of my career. I had just spent the better part of three years co-founding two separate ecommerce companies, both of which went public within a year.

It was exciting, insane, and exhausting – all at the same time.

After exiting both companies, I decided to take a break from start-up life and re-invest in my consulting practice. I dipped into the savings I had just generated, to sustain myself, while undergoing a long period of personal and professional reinvention. A process that was inherently fraught with periods of indecision, wallowing in self-doubt, changing my mind three times a week, questioning what I was doing – and so on.

I spun my wheels for months before finally seeking outside counsel; a decision that pushed me forward to where I am today. And that decision to invest in myself, to acquire objectivity, and to keep pushing forward – was inspired by one idea.

I was lying in bed one night, unable to sleep, scrolling through Instagram – like a vacant teenager at a bus stop – when suddenly, as if sent from the heavens, I came across an individual describing a model called The Emotional Cycles of Change.

As I sat there listening, I quickly perked up in my bed. This man was describing the exact emotional situation I was struggling with. Feelings I hadn't shared with anyone.

I was thunderstruck. I knew my phone could listen to me speak, but could it also read my mind?

This model changed my perspective on what it takes to be an entrepreneur. What it means to believe in yourself, to invest in yourself, to fight through adversity – and to stay committed when things become difficult.

I've therefore chosen to conclude this book by passing that model forward to you.

The Emotional Cycles of Change

The Emotional Cycles of Change was first developed by Elisabeth Kubler-Ross in her book "On Death and Dying" from 1969. A model that has been adopted and re-adapted in various ways over the years. In fact, it would be difficult for me to pinpoint which version of the model I'm sharing here, beyond giving credit to its originator.

This model describes the five emotional stages people go through when starting something new or intentionally embarking on a significant change in their lives.

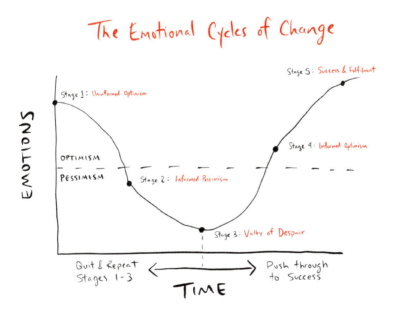

Stage 1: Uninformed Optimism

You're about to embark on something new – a big change. You're excited, although you have no idea what it'll entail or how difficult it'll be. You're optimistic, but uninformed.

Stage 2: Informed Pessimism

You get deeper into the process and start to realize how difficult this change is going to be. You're now informed as to what the change will require – but you become more and more pessimistic as you realize how difficult it's going to be. You're informed, but pessimistic.

Stage 3: The Valley of Despair

You reach an all-time low. The change now appears so difficult that you're unsure if you want to continue. Failure seems imminent. You're in the valley of despair where most people choose to give up. Only to later repeat this same process with a different attempt at change. One that sees them ending up back in the valley of despair, where they again decide to give up. A repeating cycle of attempted change and failure.

Stage 4: Informed Optimism

A small percentage of people survive the valley of despair; pushing through the most difficult stage of change to come out the other side and land at "informed optimism." You've survived the hardest part, you fully understand what is required to succeed, and you now believe you can do it. You're informed about what is required and optimistic about the end result.

Stage 5: Success & Fulfillment

You keep working and ultimately achieve your end result. You achieve success and fulfillment.

That night, lying in bed... I was in the valley of despair.

I was seriously questioning if I wanted to continue doing what I was doing. And I was close to changing course. This model gave me a new perspective. It showed me exactly where I was. In a place I had been many, many times before – but had never fully recognized.

I was in the valley of despair.

This understanding illuminated my path forward – showing me exactly what I had to do. To fight through the valley of despair and keep working toward success and fulfillment – which is exactly what I did.

You may not be in the valley of despair at this exact moment, but I guarantee you've been there before. And I can guarantee you'll be there again.

Change is never easy, but often necessary. As a leader, your true power is rooted in your ability to lead people through change. To understand how difficult it will be. To recognize where you are in the process as you go. And to have the resilience to fight through the valley of despair on the road to success and fulfillment.

It's been my pleasure keeping your attention for this long, and I hope you've enjoyed the journey.

Until next time, I wish you nothing but success in all of your endeavors, both personal and professional.

Sincerely,

Anthony Gindin

Over the past 23 years, Anthony has built six companies, published two books, spoken at events around the world, worked with executive leaders in 17 countries and been recognized with 11 international marketing awards.

As an agency veteran, Anthony has closed over $43M in agency new business and financing. While more recently, Anthony co-founded two ecommerce companies, both of which went public on the CSE within a year (before achieving successful exits). He then found himself pondering retirement at the ripe age of 39… before quickly realizing how ridiculous that idea was (and that he probably didn't have enough money yet to actually do so).

Today, Anthony devotes himself to helping agency principals systemize repeatable growth. His fulfillment comes in helping others build incredible brands, scale their businesses, and find their own ways to contribute to the success of others.

Anthony works from his home base in Canada, where he lives with his wonderful family :)

AnthonyGindin.com

Get In Touch

If you're interested in Anthony's agency growth programs or other services, please visit:

AnthonyGindin.com

Anthony Gindin

Made in the USA
Middletown, DE
21 May 2024